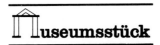

useumsstück

The Old Masters
Picture Gallery
in Dresden

The Old Masters Picture Gallery in Dresden

Harald Marx
Gregor JM Weber

Deutscher Kunstverlag

Translated from the German by
Dorothy Ann Schade-Maurice, Berlin

Photographs
All colour photographs by Jürgen Karpinski, Dresden,
except for the following:
p 88: Sächsische Landesbibliothek,
Abt. Deutsche Fotothek, Reinecke;
pp 95, 97, 99: Reinhold, Leipzig-Mölkau
Black-and-white photographs:
Staatliche Kunstsammlungen Dresden,
except for p 9: Dieter Krull, Dresden

Frontispiece
Louis de Silvestre, King August III as Prince.
Around 1718

You will find a plan of the gallery
inside the back cover.

Editor
Elisabeth Motz

Production
Anette Klinge

Reproduction
Depar, Verona (colour)
Repro Knopp Inning/Ammersee (black-and-white)

Type set by
Fotosatz Leingärtner, Nabburg

Printed by
Hofmann-Druck, Augsburg

Bound by
Großbuchbinderei Monheim, Monheim

2nd revised English edition 1997
© 1997, Deutscher Kunstverlag Munich Berlin
ISBN 3-422-06202-5

History of the Old Masters Picture Gallery in Dresden

»… Anyone wishing to travel in order to see architecture, painting and sculpture, need go no further than here. The palace houses a far larger quantity of the most beautiful statues of Antiquity, and the most splendid Netherlandish and Italian paintings, than even the Palais Royal in Paris which itself has a considerable number. In toto, this is the perfect place.« This enthusiasm about Dresden and its famous art collections, expressed by Crown Prince Frederick of Mecklenburg-Schwerin in a letter dated 1739, followed in a long line of similar views that continues to this day.

In the first half of the 18th century, paintings served a representative purpose at court. The Dresden collection was determined by the interest in art of two kings: August the Strong (1670-1733; Elector of Saxony from 1694, King of Poland from 1697), who was also keen on decorative arts, and his son and successor August III (1696-1763; Elector and King from 1733) who preferred fine arts, paintings, prints and drawings and, indeed, showed remarkable connoisseurship in these fields. Together, father and son acquired, in a little more than 50 years, all the old masters we admire in the Gallery today.

The collection's tradition is far longer than the Gallery's history. The electoral Kunstkammer, a universal collection claiming to be of encyclopaedic value, was founded in 1560. Paintings tended to play a subordinate role in this collection of items demonstrating nature, science, history, technology and art. A few important pictures were bought in the 17th century, but it was only under August the Strong that their numbers increased and special collections were created. The early 18th century saw the establishment, inter alia, of the »Grüne Gewölbe« (the Green Vault), the Sculpture Collection, and the Prints Cabinet, and then – mainly under August III – attention was paid to increasing substantially the holdings of paintings.

The works of art were purchased all over Europe, in Italy, Paris, Amsterdam and Prague. Count Heinrich Brühl, the Prime Minister of King August III, and Count Brühl's secretary, Carl Heinrich von Heinecken, arranged the purchases. Only the outbreak of the Seven Years' War, in 1756, interrupted the flow of paintings to Dresden. The acquisition of the hundred best pictures from the collection of the Duke of Modena in 1745, and the »Sistine Madonna« in 1754, deserves special mention. The taste of the 18th century, its likes and dislikes, determined the character of this Gallery. Mature styles of painting, the High Renaissance and Baroque, and virtuoso 18th century were preferred to the early phases, such as the Italian quattrocento or early Netherlandish painting. The Gallery was famous for its abundance of Italian old masters, and Dutch and Flemish painters, including numerous so-called Little Masters. German painting was also represented by Dürer and his contemporaries, although more out of respect for the former greatness of German art than out of appreciation of the paintings' artistic value.

As the collection grew with each new acquisition, and particularly with the purchase of the paintings from Modena, so did the need for a change in their accommodation. In the foreword to the Gallery's catalogue of 1826 we read: »The paintings used to hang throughout the royal apartments and palaces, but after the arrival of the works from Modena, the king wanted the paintings to be united at a single location, and ordered the building in which they are now housed, but had been constructed for another purpose, to be altered for the paintings. The building was completed in 1747, and then the paintings were hung here.« Johann Christoph Knöffel was responsible for planning and supervising the alterations to the building mentioned here, the Stall-gebäude am Jüdenhofe. When they were completed, the collection was opened to the public; a sensation at that time. Johann Joachim Winckelmann praised August III: »It is an eternal memorial to the greatness of this monarch that the greatest treasures from Italy, and works of art from other countries, should be on display, for all the world to see, in the interest of cultivating good taste.« In 1753 and 1757 two volumes were published with prints of important paintings, and in 1765 a catalogue came out in French.

A visit to the Gallery became a much-described educational experience. Many will have similar memories of the solemn nature of the collection to those of Johann Wolf-gang von Goethe: »My astonishment was far greater than I had imagined possible. The central hall in which splendour and purity prevailed in the greatest of calm, the dazzling frames, all reminding us of the time when they were gilded, the waxed floor, the rooms used more by viewers than by copyists, all conveyed a unique sense of so-lemnity such as one experiences when entering a house of God. Like the decoration of a temple, the objects of adoration seemed to be on display solely for the veneration of art.«

The change in taste at the beginning of the 19th century was accompanied by criti-cism, particularly of the full, decorative way the paintings were hung. The Berlin art scholar Alois Hirt remarked in 1830: »There is no denying that the gallery building has something noble and splendid about it (with the exception of the common en-trance). One proceeds, at a leisurely pace, in the large, broad corridors illuminated by high windows on all sides. But anyone wishing to see the paintings will notice many a disadvantage. Some of the pictures one would like to see hang too high, beyond the reach of normal vision. Sometimes the light crosses at so many different angles that one seeks, in vain, the right place to stand, with favourable illumination, for one or other painting. [...] The works of one and the same master are hung, almost mischie-vously, at great distances from one another, like a puzzle and examination for the view-er.« The unfavourable conservation conditions also caused concern. In his remarks »On the State of the Royal Painting Gallery in Dresden«, Johann Gottlob von Quandt wrote in 1842: »After several years of observation I was aware of the highly negative influence of the Gallery's damp and narrow courtyard; the air being even worse in summer than in winter. The paintings then hang in the atmosphere of a cellar.« Quandt appealed to the gallery officials' sense of responsibility, not only towards the state of Saxony, saying that »the state itself has a duty to all civilized peoples because man has a justified right to works of art of such great spiritual value.«

Thus, alterations to take account of the new aesthetic, artistic and conservational standards were unavoidable. In 1836 a »Gallery Committee« was appointed and »commissioned to examine the state of affairs.« This committee chose Gottfried Semper as the architect responsible for planning. Between 1838 and 1845 he developed various plans and models for the new museum building. After protracted discussion of the individual building concepts, Gottfried Semper's gallery building was constructed, on the northern side of the Zwinger, between 1847 and 1855.

The entrance to the building is below a flat dome – which was not planned by Semper in this form – through a three-arched portal which provides a view of the Baroque Crown Gate of the Zwinger. A domed hall, which cannot be seen from outside, leads to the Gallery on one side and (today) to the Armoury on the other. The form of the portal is reminiscent of an ancient triumphal arch; in this case celebrating the triumph of the arts. The two-storey facade displays mainly Renaissance forms. Programmatic sculptures glorify the art and poetry of Antiquity on the Theaterplatz side, and of modern times on the Zwinger side.

On the main floor, tapestries were hung in the rotunda above the entrance; the Neapolitan and Spanish paintings, then the Netherlandish and German paintings being hung in the east, and the Italian masters in the west wing. The main halls were complemented by cabinets with pictures from the same schools.

Purchasing activities began again in the mid-19th century, concentrating on contemporary pictures at first. These were to form the basis of today's Gallery of Modern Masters. Purchases of old masters aimed to close existing gaps. Thus, the Gallery acquired fifteen 17th century Spanish paintings from the estate of the Citizen King Louis Philippe of France who had been forced to abdicate in 1848 and had died in exile in London. At that time, Germany was hardly aware of the existence of Spanish art. Several excellent paintings by Italian and Netherlandish masters were added to the collection in the 1870s and 1880s.

As at other galleries, the directors were, for a long time, artists, some of whom taught at the Dresden Academy of Art. The Gallery's influence on the Academy's students should not be underestimated. Beginning with Karl Woermann, art historians were appointed as directors from 1882. This was extremely important for the scientific study of the holdings and their publication in catalogues.

At the beginning of the 20th century, alterations were made to keep pace with changing requirements. Some parts of the Gallery of Modern Masters were moved. In addition, new artistic and aesthetic demands gave rise to fundamental criticism of Semper's building. For example, Hans Posse, the Gallery's director from 1910 to 1942, criticized the lighting and room height, wall decorations and wall coverings. As a result, the vaulting in the halls was reduced to its present form, and the glass ceiling was lowered. Posse described the old decorative appearance of the halls as »ugly depot-like filling of the walls«, while Woermann, in his memoirs of 1924, warned against going to the other extreme of the »neurasthenic taste of an aesthete«. He added: »The hanging of even two pictures one above the other often met with disapproval. Indeed, it soon became the norm to demand a special section of wall for almost every picture.« Each age experiences changes in taste. Not surprisingly, therefore, today's problem is (still) to meet the requirements of the present without disregarding, or even destroying, the achievements of the past.

The Gallery came under serious threat, and was almost destroyed, when the Nazis were in power. In 1937, so-called »Entartete Kunst« (degenerate art) was removed, and the Gallery was closed, in 1938 and 1939, even before Hitler's occupation of the Sudetenland and his march into Poland. In 1942, the paintings had to be taken to a number of depots in Saxony.

Dresden was destroyed on February 13th 1945. The Zwinger and the Semper Gallery were badly damaged. When the Red Army entered the city, a military division, called the »Trophy Commission«, was ordered to look through the holdings of the Dresden collections and to select works for transport to Moscow and Kiev. No one in Germany could afford to express surprise. For ten years, the paintings seemed to have disappeared from Dresden forever. No one was allowed to mention them. Once the German Democratic Republic was considered a safe part of the Soviet sphere of influence, political conditions were created that permitted a generous gesture. On August 25th 1955, the paintings were handed over to a government delegation of the GDR in Moscow. Only then did the legend arise that the removal of the works of art from Dresden was a »rescue operation by Soviet troops«. The words of the Soviet soldier Chanutin, written in chalk on the portal: »Museum inspected. No mines« were often quoted, and the letters redrawn, but a historical examination of the events was a taboo. This should now be rectified. For Hermann Voss, Director of the Gallery from 1942 to 1945, the ultimate loss of the paintings had become »a sad certainty after co-operating, for days, with the Russian Trophy Commission« ... »No Russian officer ever said, at the time, that these steps were being taken for conservation purposes.« In 1963 the State Art Collections listed, in a catalogue entitled »War Losses of the Dresden Paintings Gallery«, what had really been lost during the war: 206 works are listed as destroyed, and 507 as missing, 44 of which have been found again in the meantime.

The Dresden Gallery was reopened on June 3rd 1956. Admirably, Semper's building was reconstructed in two phases, in 1956 and 1960, despite the extreme shortage of funds in the 1950s. Admittedly, many features were simplified, but no attempts were made to change radically Semper's style of architecture. With the Gallery's reconstruction Dresden recovered part of its identity. Since the city's destruction, many people in Dresden have lived with two realities, the past and the present; a life with pictures. The Gallery began to stand for hope, and pictures of it began to replace what had been lost. Thus, the memory of the Dresden of Bernardo Bellotto lives to this day.

As time passed, the state of the gallery building deteriorated, and from 1976 the Director of the Gallery, and the Director General of the Dresden Museums, called for measures to be taken. After an alarming expertise on the building, the Gallery was finally, and overhastily, closed on February 16th 1988. First of all, the technical problems had to be solved. Priority was given to carrying out the necessary repairs to the roof, facades, windows and cellars, and to renewing the electrical installations, security systems, heating, air-conditioning and lighting in the exhibition rooms.

The reconstruction concept also addressed the question of the Gallery's future appearance. Gottfried Semper's famous museum building was to be respected, and re-

Semper Gallery, three-arched portal

stored, as far as possible; an aim on which museum specialists, experts on the preservation of historic monuments, and architects agreed. They had to reconcile the needs of the historic building with those of a modern museum. In addition, they had to recognize that alterations had also been made, for a variety of reasons, in the 20th century, and these cannot simply be erased without a trace.

The visitor now finds a completely renewed building which has nevertheless retained its historic character. Ticket desks and cloakrooms have been moved from the entrance hall to make it more spacious again, and the highly decorative grisaille paintings and narrative reliefs, that were painted over or removed in the mid-1950s, have been restored.

Today, respect for Semper and his architectural achievement demands that the hanging of the paintings takes account of the rooms' dimensions. This meant striking a balance between recreating the 19th century museum as an architectural masterpiece and meeting the requirements of a modern museum.

When the pictures were hung close together, a strong deep overall shade predominated, when the paintings were spaced more generously the colour of the wall became more apparent. Therefore, a deep red was chosen for the Italian, and a soft green for the Netherlandish department, as in Leo von Klenze's design for the Alte Pinakothek in Munich. The walls of the entrance hall and the centre rooms with French and Spanish paintings are in different shades of grey, as if to mediate between the red and the green.

The purpose and function of such a Gallery today was also questioned. For Dresden, a city that suffered such painful losses both during the war and the decades that followed, a solution had to be found which keeps history alive and thus upholds the museum tradition. Gottfried Semper's architecture and the paintings set very high standards of value. The paintings of the old masters express different fates and hopes, experiences and dreams of past ages; they mirror our own history. Thus, as Julius Hübner knew in 1856, the Gallery will become, once again, »A destination for pious pilgrims of all nations.«

Bibliography

on the Gallery's history and the individual paintings in: Gemäldegalerie Dresden. Alte Meister. Katalog der ausgestellten Werke. 8th revised and completed edition 1992

Pinturicchio
(Bernardino di Betto Biagio)

Perugia c. 1454-Siena 1513

Portrait of a Boy
Poplar, 50 x 35.5 cm
First mentioned in the inventory of
1722-1728.
Gal. no. 41

In 1722, this work was believed to be the portrait of the young Raphael. This cannot be
proved, but Pinturicchio was certainly influenced by Raphael's teacher, Perugino, under
whom he worked on the frescoes in the Sistine
Chapel in Rome in 1481/83. This delicate
portrait of a boy, set against a clear morning
landscape to emphasize the youth's character,
must have been painted in this period. The
portrait was not painted in oils but in very
watery tempera so that the forms could be
shaped in numerous parallel strokes.

14

Andrea Mantegna

Isola di Cartura near Piazzola c. 1431-
Mantua 1506

Holy Family
Canvas, 75 x 61.5 cm
Acquired in 1876. Gal. no. 51

Mantegna's highly sculpted art marks the transition from the Early to the High Renaissance. He was court painter to the Gonzaga family in Mantua from 1459. The *Holy Family*, painted around 1485 or perhaps at the end of the 15th century, is reminiscent of reliefs of Antiquity, in which the juxtaposition of figures of the same height was a principle of composition. The severely sculptured heads to the right and left of the Madonna seem to have been modelled on realistic Roman portrait busts, while the greater grace of Mary and the Christ Child suggests Florentine reliefs of the Early Renaissance, such as those of Luca della Robbia. The infant St John the Baptist (lower right) indicates, with his gesture and banderole, Christ as the Lamb of God, and thus points to the Passion of the Saviour. It is unknown whether the figures on Mary's right and left are St Elisabeth, John's mother, and St Joseph, Christ's foster-father, or Mary's parents Joachim and Anne.

Francesco del Cossa ▷

Ferrara 1435/36-Bologna 1477/78

Annunciation
Poplar, 137.5 x 113 cm
Acquired in 1750. Gal. no. 43

When this altarpiece came to Dresden in 1750, it was thought to be Mantegna's work because of its clear lines and highly sculpted forms. However, Cossa was also influenced by the works of Cosimo Tura and Piero della Francesca. This major work was painted shortly after 1470 when Cossa had moved from Ferrara to Bologna. It shows the Archangel Gabriel telling the Virgin Mary that she will bear the Son of God (St Luke 1: 26-38). Above the angel, the painting shows God the Father sending the Holy Spirit (represented by a dove), and below, on the predella, the Nativity. The two figures on the main panel are framed by the richly ornamented architecture as if they were two separate pictures.

Sandro Botticelli
(Alessandro Filipepi)

Florence 1444/45-Florence 1510

Four Scenes from the Life of St Zenobius
Poplar, 66 x 186 cm
Acquired in 1868. Gal. no. 9

The importance of drawing for the Florentine School is particularly obvious in the works of Botticelli whose figures are brought to life by their rhythmically drawn outlines. This panel shows scenes from the life of St Zenobius, the bishop and patron saint of Florence who died in 417. There are two further panels in the National Gallery, London, and another one in the Metropolitan Museum of Art, New York. They were probably ordered as a »spalliere«, a frieze of shoulder-height pictures, by Francesco de Girolamo for the marriage of his son Zanobi in 1500. The bishop and saint was thought to be the family's ancestor. As in earlier art, the panel in Dresden shows simultaneously different scenes of the last miracle performed by the saint. On the left, a boy is run over by a cart, to the horror of his parents. In the next scene, the boy is brought to Deacon Eugenio who, thanks to the miraculous powers of Zenobius, heals the boy and gives him back to his parents (centre). On the right, the saint blesses a group of bishops and monks from his deathbed.

Lorenzo di Credi

Florence c. 1458-Florence 1537

Holy Family
Poplar, 87.5 x 65 cm
Acquired in 1874. Gal. no. 14

This Florentine artist came from the workshop of the sculptor and painter Andrea del Verocchio who was also the teacher of Leonardo da Vinci. The accurately drawn contours, fine details and severity of the architecture link his art with the Early Renaissance. Mary adoring the Christ Child dominates the foreground, while a small figure of Joseph is seated in the landscape behind the arch on the right. The ears of wheat on which the Child is lying symbolize the body of Christ in the form of the Host, the goldfinch the human soul, and the dandelion the Passion.

Francesco Francia
(Francesco Raibolini)

Bologna c. 1450-Bologna 1517/18

Adoration of the Magi
Poplar, 41 x 59 cm
First mentioned in the inventory of 1754.
Gal. no. 49

The Bolognese painter Francia was influenced by the art of Ferrara, for he was a pupil of Lorenzo Costa who had moved from Ferrara to Bologna. Francia was also interested in the works of Lorenzo di Credi and Perugino. The latter's influence is particularly obvious in the *Adoration of the Magi* which, upon its acquisition in the mid-18th century, was believed to be the work of Raphael's teacher. This impression is created largely by the fine contours of dominant figures and forms which make the painting so graceful. It depicts a theme from the New Testament (St Matthew 2: 9-11). The Three Wise Men from the East had come to Jerusalem to pay homage to the King of the Jews because they had seen his star on high. They followed the star until it came to a halt over Bethlehem where they found the Christ Child.

Cima da Conegliano
(Giovanni Battista Cima)

Conegliano 1459/60-Conegliano 1517/18

Presentation of the Virgin at the Temple
Poplar, 105 x 145 cm
First mentioned in the inventory of 1754.
Gal. no. 63

From 1492 to 1516 Cima worked in Venice. There he painted his *Presentation of the Virgin at the Temple* shortly before 1500. In accordance with an apocryphal gospel, it shows Mary, as a three-year-old child, being taken by her parents to the temple where she is to lead a life in the service of God until she is married. The painting's charm is due to its splendid colours and poetic transfiguration, combined with the artist's delight in details of everyday life. Following in the footsteps of Gentile Bellini and Carpaccio, Cima included realistic secondary scenes, such as the egg seller and the little birdseller, in his treatment of this theme. Among other things, these scenes were to in-

fluence Titian when he painted his version of the same theme a generation later (Gallerie dell' Accademia, Venice).

Antonello da Messina

Messina c. 1450-Messina 1479

St Sebastian
Transfererd from wood to canvas,
171 x 85.5 cm
Acquired in 1873. Gal. no 52

The surprisingly tall figure of St Sebastian rises up in front of us, his expression transfigured. The physical pain of his martyrdom no

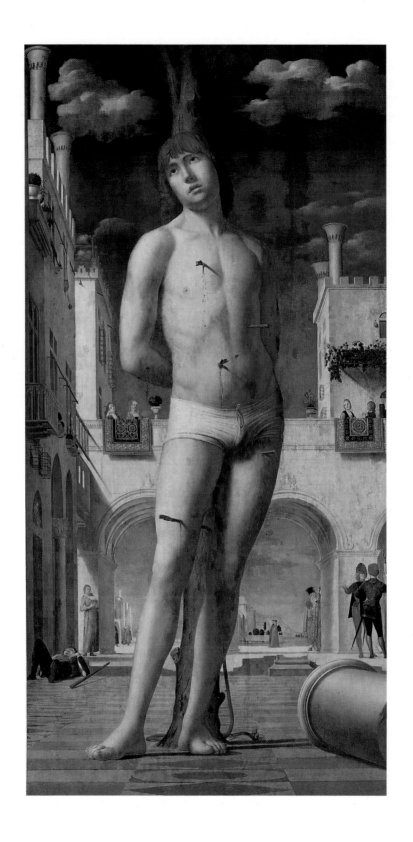

longer seems to affect him as he turns his thoughts to the hereafter. His body, pierced by arrows, reminds us of the balanced proportions of the statues of Antiquity. The figure looks extraordinarily tall because Antonello uses the centralized perspective to locate the vanishing point behind the saint's knees. The lines of the floor and buildings taper rapidly towards the horizon, making the saint in the foreground look all the more monumental. As a result, the extremely small secondary figures are in exactly calculable positions. In addition to these exemplary innovations, Antonello is thought to have introduced, to Italy, the Netherlandish painting technique of using oil, rather than tempera, as a binder. He was, therefore, an innovator, even in Venice where he painted *St Sebastian* in 1475/76.

Giorgione (Giorgio da Castelfranco)

Castelfranco 1477/78-Venice 1510

Sleeping Venus
Canvas, 108.5 x 175 cm
Acquired in 1699. Gal. no. 185

When Marc Antonio Michiel saw Giorgione's picture in Venice in 1525, he wrote in his journal that Titian had completed the landscape and added Cupid. Giorgione had died, at an early age, of the plague in 1510, so it seemed obvious that his friend and fellow pupil of Giovanni Bellini should complete the unfinished work. Today, Titian's contribution is believed to be the group of buildings on the right and the flow of drapery on which Venus lies. The scanty remains of a small Cupid at Venus' feet were covered over in 1837/43, but he can still be seen on X-rays. Cupid's presence is not required to recognize the sleeping figure as Venus, since she is represented as a *Venus pudica* after models of Antiquity. The ideal beauty of her peacefully stretched-out body, the likes of which had not been painted before, was to inspire many generations of artists. However, few painters were ever to achieve such poetic harmony between the human body and the landscape: »The soft undulating contours of her body are reiterated in the hills on the horizon, the evening calm comes down on the landscape like sleep on Venus.« (Götz Pochat, 1973).

Altobello Meloni

Worked in Cremona c. 1497-1518

Lovers
Poplar, 52 x 71.5 cm
Acquired in 1746. Gal. no. 221

This work was attributed to Giorgione as early as 1618 in Modena, from where it was purchased for the Dresden Gallery in 1746. Later is was attributed to Romanino, a painter from Brescia who influenced Meloni. It was only in 1957 that Mina Gregori produced convincing evidence of Meloni's authorship. The painting certainly conveys some of Giorgione's lyricism in its powerful portrayal of a lansquenet and his courtesan, which can be described neither as a conventional double portrait nor as pure genre. The man's aloof and disdainful look helps the viewer to understand why a weaker version of this painting, in the Budapest Museum, used to be considered a self-portrait of Giorgione with his mistress.

Titian (Tiziano Vecellio) ▷

Pieve di Cadore probably c. 1488/90-Venice 1576

Virgin and Child with Four Saints
Poplar, 138 x 191 cm
Acquired in 1747. Gal. no. 168

Titian's art ranges from the lyricism of Giorgione, through the ideality of the High Renaissance to the expressiveness of Mannerism. As the leading representative of the Venetian School, which gave precedence to colour rather than drawing, he provided important bases for European painting. The Dresden Gallery owns three portraits and two religious paintings by Titian: His *Virgin and Child with Four Saints* was painted around 1516 in the old form of a *Sacra Conversazione*. It shows, in »holy conversation«, figures from the Bible and church history, not in a historical setting but as advocates for a specific devotional purpose. Apart from the Virgin, the saints in this picture – John the Baptist, the apostle Paul, the penitent Magdalene and Jerome – all changed their way of life and repented; a course of action which they advocated or exemplified.

Titian (Tiziano Vecellio)

Pieve di Cadore probably c. 1488/90-Venice 1576

Tribute Money
Inscribed on right on Pharisee's collar:
TICIANVS.F.
Poplar, 75 x 56 cm
Acquired in 1746. Gal. no. 169

The Pharisees wanted to cause Christ's downfall by asking him a trick question (St Matthew 22: 15-22). As the Jews were suffering because of the high taxes levied by the Romans, the Pharisees sent alleged disciples to Jesus to ask whether or not it was lawful to pay tribute to Caesar? However, he saw through their trick, asked to be shown a coin, pointed to the image of the emperor and to the inscription and replied: »Render therefore unto Caesar the things which are Caesar's; and unto God the things that are God's«. Titian summarizes the entire story in a dramatic composition of two very different heads and hands. The expressive power of an angular profile and a gnarled hand contrasts with that of an ideally proportioned face which, for that very reason, does not permit any ambiguous interpretations. This early work was painted around 1516 for Duke Alfonso I d'Este of Ferrara who also commissioned other masterpieces by Titian. ▷

Palma Vecchio
(Jacopo d'Antonio de Negreti)

Serinalta near Bergamo c. 1480-Venice 1528

Jacob and Rachel
Inscribed in foreground on sack: G.B.F.
Canvas, 146.5 x 250.5 cm
First mentioned in the Guarienti inventory
(1747-1750). Gal. no. 192

Jacob was told, by his father, to look for a wife among the daughters of his uncle Laban. According to Genesis 29: 1-12, after a long journey Jacob met some shepherds at a well with a huge stone at its mouth. This was not removed until all the flocks had gathered. When Rachel, Laban's daughter, arrived with her father's sheep, Jacob watered the flock and »kissed Rachel, and lifted up his voice, and wept«. Jacob's love was so great that he served his uncle fourteen years for Rachel. Palma Vecchio sets this touching scene in a broad pastoral landscape of earthy colours and soft light, with flocks and pastures. Giorgione's strong influence can also be seen in Palma's painting, created in Venice around 1515-20.

Lorenzo Lotto

Venice c. 1480-Loreto 1556

Virgin and Child with the Infant St John the Baptist

Inscribed on left on edge of wall:
Laurentius Lotus 15.8 [1518]
Poplar, 52 x 39 cm
First mentioned in the 1765 catalogue.
Gal. no. 194 A

Lotto's life as a wanderer frequently took him away from Venice. He was inspired by the art he saw on his travels, and was even interested in art north of the Alps. During his stay in Rome in 1509, he became familiar with Raphael's work; a significant experience. Lotto painted this intimate picture of the Virgin in 1518. He was in Bergamo at the time, since he wanted to see the Lombard painting influenced by Leonardo da Vinci. The Madonna's delicate face is reminiscent of works by Leonardo's successors, Giampietrino or Andrea Solario, whose circle also used the motif of the two children caressing one another. Nevertheless, Lotto's painting is more than a combination of other artists' motifs. It is a synthesis tempered by his individual sense of colour.

Raphael (Raffaello Santi)

Urbino 1483-Rome 1520

Sistine Madonna
Canvas, 269.5 x 201 cm
Acquired in 1753/54. Gal. no. 93

The Dresden Gallery's reputation is linked inseparably with Raphael's masterpiece. At the same time, it was here that the painting attained its undying fame. It could not have achieved such status without the concept of Classicism, such as was created by Winckelmann and Mengs, or without the humanistic educational ideal of the Enlightenment which found the culture of the Italian High Renaissance concentrated, in exemplary fashion, in this work. Its exhibition in a public gallery, and its dissemination in countless reproductions, resulted in the painting's immense popularity. Nevertheless, the splendour of this work, which is often concealed by its very fame, can still be discovered anew. – Commissioned by Pope Julius II, Raphael painted this picture for the main altar of the Monastery Church of San Sisto in Piacenza in 1512/13. The painting is named after the titular saint of the church, Pope Sixtus, who died a martyr in the 3rd century. He appears, on the left, as a mediator between the Madonna and the faithful in front of the picture, for whom he asks her divine mercy with a gesture of the hand. The acorn on the top of the tiara (lower left) indicates the painting's donor, it being part of the coat of arms of the della Rovere family to which Pope Julius II belonged. The features of St Sixtus also resemble that pope. His family showed special reverence for St Barbara who was martyred in the 3rd century. She is kneeling on the left of the picture. Her attribute, a tower in which she was held captive, can be seen behind her shoulder. Elevated between these two saints, the Madonna with Child is aureoled by very faintly painted heads of angels. Two far more corporeal angels lean on the balustrade in the foreground which, like the draped curtains above, creates a link between our earthly surroundings and the heavenly being. The position of each form, each motif, has been determined, and cannot be altered, in this harmonious triangular composition. The gestures and attitudes of the figures are finely coordinated, and the framework encourages the viewer to contemplate. With its human scale yet majestic solemnity, the painting exudes a harmony which makes it one of Raphael's most perfect creations.

Dosso Dossi (Giovanni di Luteri)

Probably Ferrara c. 1489-Ferrara c. 1542

Battista Dossi (Battista di Luteri)

Probably Ferrara c. 1493/95-Ferrara 1548

St George
Canvas, 206 x 121 cm
Acquired in 1746. Gal. no. 124

The painting by the two Dossi brothers is modelled on a far smaller composition by Raphael (c. 1505/06, National Gallery, Washington). The brothers' joint authorship is substantiated by payments by the treasury of Duke Ercole II d'Este in Ferrara in 1540. The Dossi brothers transform the bright landscape of Raphael's painting into a dramatically sombre backdrop with strong contrasts of light and dark. In this picture, Raphael's influence is combined with Venetian elements, notably Giorgione's. St George slayed a dragon to which a king's daughter was to be sacrificed, thus becoming a symbol of the victory of good over evil. This is also shown in a pendant of the Archangel Michael fighting Satan (Gal. no. 125).

Andrea del Sarto (Andrea d'Agnolo) ▷

Florence 1486-Florence 1530

The Sacrifice of Abraham
Inscribed in foreground on stone with
monogram AA (linked)
Poplar, 213 x 159 cm
Acquired in 1746. Gal. no. 77

This dramatic painting shows the moment at which the greatest of tragedies turns to happiness. God wanted to test Abraham's faith and ordered him to sacrifice his own son as a burnt offering. At the very last moment an angel tells Abraham to stop what he is doing. Instead he kills a ram caught in a thicket by his horns (Genesis 22: 1-13). Vasari, reporting on the picture for King François I of France, is delighted by the »beautiful, delicate boy Isaac« who, »completely naked, trembles in fear of death«. Andrea del Sarto had been impressed by the ancient Laocoon group excavated in 1506, to which this work, completed shortly before his death, owes as much as to the art of Michelangelo.

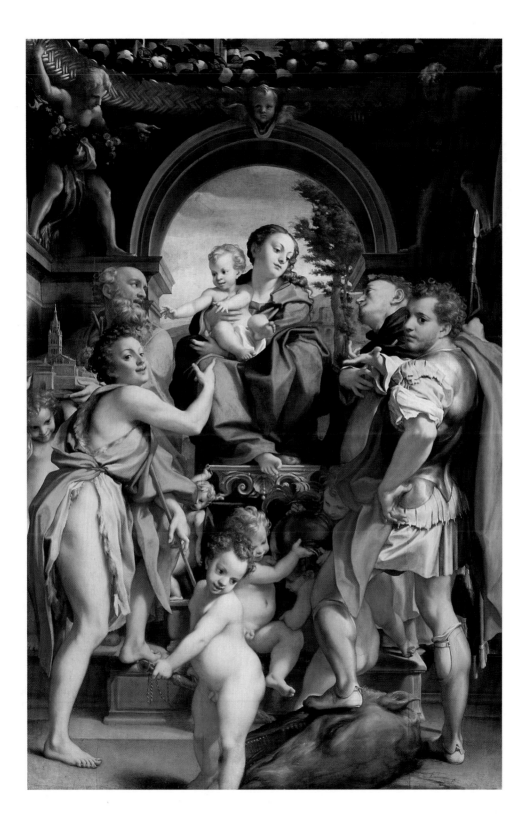

◁ Correggio (Antonio Allegri)

Correggio c. 1489-Correggio 1534

Madonna with St George
Poplar, 285 x 190 cm
Acquired in 1746. Gal. no. 153

Nowhere outside Italy can Correggio be studied better than in the Dresden Gallery, the proud owner of four of his large altarpieces. The *Madonna with St George* was painted in 1530/32 for the brethren of San Pietro Martire in Modena. It is a *Sacra Conversazione*, with the Madonna enthroned and surrounded by four saints. On the left, John the Baptist points to the infant Jesus who, for his part, is reaching out for a model of Modena held by Bishop Geminianus. On the right, the martyr Peter (of Verona), the brethren's patron saint, asks for the Madonna's intercession. St George stands in the foreground with the dragon he has slain, while several putti play with his heavy arms. The painting in brilliant colours displays such a surprisingly high degree of »grazia e delicatezza« that it was still to serve as a model for Rococo artists two centuries later.

Parmigianino (Girolamo Francesco Maria Mazzola)

Parma 1503-Casalmaggiore near Parma 1540

Madonna of the Rose
Poplar, 109 x 88.5 cm
Acquired in 1752. Gal. no. 161

Although Parmigianino was greatly influenced by Correggio in Parma, he developed his own Mannerist style which is characterized by exquisite elegance, flowing lines and unusual colours. The *Madonna della Rosa* possesses all these qualities to perfection. It was painted in 1528/30 in Bologna for Pietro Aretino, a man of letters, but – according to Vasari – was then given to Pope Clement VII. The ambivalence of such a picture of the Madonna, which could equally portray Venus and Amor, makes it »Art for Art's Sake« rather than a devotional picture. The iconoclastic controversy had begun. Calvin, for example, found the prostitutes in brothels more chaste than the pictures of virgins on display in the churches (*Institutio* III: 28).

Daniele da Volterra (Daniele Ricciarelli)

Volterra (Province of Pisa) 1509-Rome 1566

Moses on Mount Sinai
Poplar, 139 x 99.5 cm
First mentioned in the inventory of 1754.
Gal. no. 84

Greatly angered, Moses breaks the tables of the law he has just received from God on Mount Sinai when he sees his faithless people dancing around the golden calf (Exodus 32:19). The drama of the situation can be seen in the stretched-out figure of Moses against the dark background, and in the gestures of the horror-striken Jews pleading for forgiveness. The figures, writhing with emotion, follow the Mannerist canon of forms. Volterra is not afraid to show the same pose, from different angles, in the same picture. In this work, painted around 1545-55, the tension created by the forms corresponds with the pathos of the contents, thus marking out Volterra as the artistic successor of his friend Michelangelo.

Jacopo Bassano (Jacopo da Ponte)

Bassano (Province of Vicenza) probably 1510-Bassano 1592

Moses Smites the Rock for the Children of Israel
Canvas, 113 x 175 cm
First mentioned in the Guarienti inventory (1747-1750). Gal. no. 256

Jacopo Bassano and his four sons had a large workshop, so it is often very difficult to decide exactly which artists contributed to a particular painting. A large proportion of this work is attributed to Francesco (1549-1592). However, the canvas could have been painted by Leandros (1557-1622). Thus, the picture is unlikely to have been painted before 1580. Scenes brimful of figures in dark-coloured landscapes were among the specialities of the Bassano workshop. The biblical themes are lost in throngs of people and animals which are so reminiscent of the beautiful pastoral landscapes of Venetian painting. Here, on the left, Moses saves the children of Israel from dying of thirst by smiting a rock, from which water pours forth, upon God's order (Exodus 17:1-7).

Paolo Veronese (Paolo Caliari)

Verona 1528-Venice 1588

Adoration of the Magi
Canvas, 206 x 455 cm
Acquired in 1746. Gal. no. 225

In his large paintings, Veronese shows similar decorative abundance to Bassano, although his work is brighter, more festive and splendid. The *Adoration of the Magi* belongs, with three other pictures of almost the same size, to a series which Veronese painted for the Venetian patrician family of the Cuccina in 1571. On this frieze-like painting, groups on the left, around Mary, and on the right, around the Moorish king, order the wealth of forms and colours, heavy materials with rich patterns, exotic faces and costumes. Everything the Venetian traders had to offer from the Orient is mixed, in this painting, with the gifts, of the Magi, of gold, frankincense and myrrh (St Matthew 2: 1-12). The playful control, rather than ostentatious demonstration, of artistic means shows Veronese at the height of his skill.

Jacopo Tintoretto (Jacopo Robusti)   ▷

Venice 1518-Venice 1594

Archangel Michael Fights Satan
Canvas, 318 x 220 cm
First mentioned in the inventory of 1754.
Gal. no. 266

This late work by Tintoretto, who, with Veronese, succeeded Titian as Venice's leading painter, displays none of the calm and worldly beauty of the previous picture. Here an extreme vision of the hereafter, full of unpleasant premonitions, fears and desires, flickers in an unreal light. The figures hover, push and fall, oriented only by the diagonal thrust of Michael's lance. The prophetic words of the last book of the Bible (Revelation 12: 1-9) report the appearance of a woman in heaven – frequently equated with the Mother of God – who bears a male child who will rule all people, and the arrival of a seven-headed dragon that threatens to devour the child, but is overcome by Michael and his angels. While Tintoretto adheres largely to the text, he also displays extraordinary imagination and religious emotion.

El Greco (Domenikos Theotokopoulos)

Candia/Crete c. 1545-Toledo 1614

Healing of the Blind Man
Poplar, 65.5 x 84 cm
Acquired in 1741. Gal. no. 276

El Greco, the Greek, is inseparably linked with the art of Spain, his adopted country. Nevertheless, his *Healing of the Blind Man* is reminiscent of Tintoretto, whose late work displayed the Venetian Mannerist style which is still reflected in El Greco's early painting. As in some of Tintoretto's compositions, El Greco purposefully leaves the centre of the picture free, and creates, with the perspective, an unrealistic depth like on an inclined stage. The blind man (after St Matthew 9: 27-31) is healed on the far left, while a crowd of excited onlookers stands on the right.

Annibale Carracci ▷

Bologna 1560-Rome 1609

Madonna Enthroned with St Matthew
Inscribed on edge of tablet:
HANNIBAL CARRACTIVS BON. F.
MDLXXXVIII.
Canvas, 384 x 255 cm
Acquired in 1746. Gal. no. 304

Annibale Carracci painted this *Sacra Conversazione* in 1588 for the merchants' chapel of the Church of San Prospero in Reggio Emilia. On the left, Matthew the Evangelist and, on the right, John the Baptist stand confidently, while St Francis, in the centre, humbly kisses the infant's foot. Some motifs, such as Matthew's angel in the foreground, are reminiscent of Correggio under whose influence Carracci stood until around 1587/88. The asymmetrical

arrangement of the figures is modelled on Venetian paintings, from Veronese's *Marriage of St Catherine* of about 1575 (today Gallerie dell' Accademia, Venice) to Titian's *Pesaro Madonna* of 1526 (Frari Church, Venice). In 1588, the year the picture was painted, Carracci had visited Venice from Bologna where he ran a workshop, with his brother and cousin, which was of immense importance for the development of Baroque painting.

Reni came from the Carracci School, but had learnt with Ludovico in Bologna and was later influenced by Annibale in Rome. There, Caravaggio had introduced a completely new approach. By breaking with the Mannerist rules of style, returning to nature for models, and using strong contrasts of light and dark, he revolutionized the artistic means used in painting from 1600. The Dresden altarpiece, an early work, clearly shows the influence, on Reni, of both Carracci and Caravaggio. The painting had adorned the chapel of the shoe-makers' guild in Reggio from 1621 at the latest. This accounts for the presence, on the left, of the shoemakers' patrons SS Crispin and Crispinian. The figure of the reading hermit Paul, formerly thought to be Jerome, displays Caravaggio's strong influence.

Guido Reni

Bologna 1575-Bologna 1642

Madonna Enthroned with Three Saints
Canvas, 319 x 216 cm
Acquired in 1746. Gal. no. 328

Guercino (Giovanni Francesco Barbieri) ▷

Cento near Ferrara 1591-Bologna 1666

The Ecstasy of St Francis
Canvas, 162.5 x 127 cm
Acquired in 1756. Gal. no. 356

The artist, called »Il Guercino« (»cross-eyes«) because of his eye defect, taught himself to paint in Cento but was strongly influenced by Ludovico Carracci. During the short rule of the Bolognese Pope Gregory XV (1621-23), he rose to eminence as chief painter at the papal court. Guercino painted this *Ecstasy of St Francis* soon after returning from Rome. He had already created a similar composition, with one more figure, in 1620 (now in the Louvre in Paris). The masterly use of contrasting light and shade, revealing a knowledge of Caravaggio's innovations, unites the different parts of the picture. Guercino was later to pursue an increasingly classicistic style in reaction to Reni's further development.

Valentin de Boulogne

Coulommiers-en-Brie 1591-Rome 1632

The Cheats
Mark of collection upper right: ·L·
Canvas, 94.5 x 137 cm
Acquired in 1749. Gal. no. 408

Although Valentin was born in France, he settled in Rome at an early age, around 1612. He must have come under the direct influence of Bartolomeo Manfredi who, for his part, knew Caravaggio's art firsthand and developed it. The »Manfrediana methodus«, so named by Joachim von Sandrart in 1675/79, can be studied, in Dresden, in the *Guard Room* (Gal. no. 411) attributed to Manfredi, and in the work of Valentin and other northern Caravaggisti. The compositions, seen at close quarters with a colourful mixture of knavish demi-monde figures against a dark ground, are modelled powerfully by light from the side. Valentin's *Cheats*, painted around 1615/18, are based on a composition on the same theme by Caravaggio, to whom this painting was attributed until 1906.

Adam Elsheimer

Frankfurt am Main 1578-Rome 1610

*Jupiter and Mercury in the House of
Philemon and Baucis*
Copper, 16.5 x 22.5 cm
First mentioned in the inventory of 1754.
Gal. no. 1977

Adam Elsheimer arrived in Rome around
1600. There he painted this interior, full of atmosphere. It is among his most important
works. Ovid tells the touching story of Philemon and Baucis in his *Metamorphoses* VIII,
618 seqq. Jupiter and Mercury, two wandering
gods in disguise, were turned away from many
doors before the old married couple gave them
a warm welcome in their simple home. This
small but fine cabinet picture displays Elsheimer's personal interpretation of Caravaggio's
light effects. His poetic treatment of everyday
life was to have a large following both in Italy
and the Netherlands where the painting was
known from 1612 and popularized by en-
graved reproductions. The picture's influence
may even be seen in Rembrandt's works.
When Goethe saw, on an engraving of the
composition, that Jupiter's eyes fell on a picture, on the wall, of one of his amorous adventures, he commented: »If such a feature is
not worth more than a whole warehouse of
real antique chamberpots, then I shall give up
all thinking, composing of poetry, all aspira-
tion and writing.«

Johann Liss

Oldenburg County c. 1597-Venice 1629

Hercules' Choice
Canvas, 61 x 75 cm
Acquired in 1925. Gal. no. 1841 A

Young Hercules must choose between Virtue and Vice. According to the story in the 3rd-century *Vita Apolloni Tyanei* by Philostrates the Elder, Vice is portrayed as a radiant beauty with crimson garments, adorned with gold and jewels, while Virtue looks as if she works, is colourless and poorly dressed. And yet appearances are deceptive. In this painting, the hand of Vice points downwards, to decline, while the hand of Virtue points to heaven, the reward for human efforts. Liss was greatly impressed by the style and choice of colours of painting in Venice when he arrived there, in 1621 at the latest, after years of study in the Netherlands. This picture was painted around 1625 after a brief stay in Rome where Liss had studied Annibale Carracci's heroic portrayal of the same theme and Elsheimer's landscapes with their small figures.

Domenico Fetti

Rome 1589-Venice 1623

Parable of the Lost Coin
Poplar, 55 x 44 cm
Acquired in 1742. Gal. no. 418

Fetti's development in Rome was influenced by the work of Elsheimer and Saraceni. He moved to Mantua to become painter at the Gonzaga court in 1613, and then on to Venice in 1621. This is one of the series of Fetti's representations of biblical parables, most of which exist in several repetitions, painted during his last years in Mantua. The Dresden Gallery owns eight of the series of fourteen motifs. In the Parable of the Lost Coin (St Luke 15: 8-10) we read: »Either what woman having ten pieces of silver, if she lose one piece, doth not light a candle, and sweep the house, and seek diligently till she find it?« When viewing this natural everyday scene, it is not difficult to imagine the importance of Fetti's work for the new trend in Venetian painting after Jacopo Tintoretto and his School.

Bernardo Strozzi   ▷

Genoa 1581-Venice 1644

Female Musician with Viola da Gamba
Canvas, 126 x 99 cm
Acquired in 1743. Gal. no. 658

Towards the end of his life, Strozzi also moved to Venice. There he developed new ideas with paintings such as his *Female Musician with Viola da Gamba* (around 1635) pointing to the end of Mannerism. Previously he had worked in Genoa, and followed Caravaggio's example. Then he discovered Rubens. However, Strozzi's bristly brush stroke (a feature he shares with Ribera) and his powerful sculpted forms make his work unmistakable. The musician is believed to be the composer Barbara Strozzi, daughter of the poet Giulio Strozzi. With her melancholy expression, bare bosom and musical instruments, she resembles a muse; a source of inspiration.

Bartholomé Estéban Murillo

Seville 1618-Seville 1682

Virgin and Child
Canvas, 166 x 115 cm
Acquired in 1755. Gal. no. 705

Murillo worked almost exclusively in the town of his birth, Seville. However, he was probably in Madrid between 1648 and 1650. There he became familiar with the works of Rubens and Van Dyck, Velázquez and the 16th century Venetians. His works of religious sincerity, great simplicity and beauty made him the head of the Seville School and also one of the most celebrated artists of the Spanish High Baroque. His paintings glorifying Mary, the triumphant *Immaculata* and the more tranquil *Madonnas*, have made him famous way beyond the frontiers of Spain and beyond the 17th century. This *Virgin and Child*, painted around 1670, displays a fine sense of colour and, in its calm, self-contained form, is entirely subordinated to the religious content.

Jusepe de Ribera

Játiva (Province of Valencia) 1591-Naples 1652

St Agnes in Prison
Signed: Jusepe de Ribera español.F.1641.
Canvas, 203 x 152 cm
Acquired in 1745. Gal. no. 683

Ribera moved to Italy at an early age and finally settled in Naples in 1616. Impressed by Caravaggio, he developed a very personal style of realistic chiaroscuro painting. His pastose brushwork enabled him to paint perfectly old saints and philosophers in particular – »old, worn bodies with wrinkled skin« (Sandrart, 1675). In his late period, the artist used more colour and light than in earlier works. His interest in light effects is seen in this painting of St Agnes of 1641. According to the legend, she was stripped of her clothing during Diocletian's persecution of the Christians. Agnes wrapped her long hair around herself until an angel brought her a garment. Ribera rarely painted such a girlishly pure picture of female beauty, as is otherwise known primarily from works of the Seville School.

Diego Rodriguez de Silva y Velázquez

Seville 1599-Madrid 1660

Portrait of a Gentleman, Probably Don Juan Mateos, Royal Master of the Hunt
Canvas, 108.5 x 90 cm
Acquired in 1746. Gal. no. 697

Velázquez is one of the most outstanding portraitists of all time. After an apprenticeship with Francisco Pacheco in Seville, he first visited Madrid in 1621, and then moved to the city, in 1623, where he became court painter to King Philip IV. In 1629-31 and 1649-51 he visited Italy for study purposes. Initially, Velázquez was influenced both thematically and formally by Caravaggio, but then he developed his own great, distinctive style which, in his portraits, was reminiscent of Titian. Indeed, it was under this name that the *Portrait of a Gentleman* first came to the Dresden Gallery. In this portrait full of life, Velázquez dispenses largely with colour effects, focusing on the skilfully sculptured face. In contrast, the hands are only sketched.

49

Nicolas Poussin

Les Andelys/Normandy 1594-Rome 1665

Adoration of the Magi
Signed and dated lower right, on shaft of column:
Accad: rom. NICOLAVS PUSIN faciebat Romae.
1633
Canvas, 160 x 182 cm
Acquired in 1742. Gal. no. 717

Apart from a brief interruption in Paris in 1640-42, Poussin lived and worked in Rome from 1624. There he developed his painting under the influence of Roman art, by Raphael and Carracci, but also of Antiquity. In his paintings, Poussin aimed to find a »mode«appropriate, in form and colour, to the subject matter. As the prime representative of the classical trend within Roman Baroque painting, his influence on the artists of the French Academy was unparalleled; his style being analysed in disputes on art theory. In this *Adoration of the Magi*, the sculpted figures are set in an ideal scene, and the strong bright colours seem to be spread across the entire canvas.

Nicolas Poussin

Les Andelys/Normandy 1594-Rome 1665

The Realm of Flora
Canvas, 131 x 181 cm
First mentioned in the inventory of 1722-1728.
Gal. no. 719

Poussin consciously chooses a different mode in this amazingly luminous painting in delicate shades, produced around 1630/31. It shows the goddess Flora dancing in her garden, surrounded by mythological figures who, after death, were transformed into flowers. On the left, Clytië looks up to her beloved Apollo in his sun-chariot – she became a sunflower. In front of her, Narcissus gazes, full of love, at his own reflection in the water which the water nymph holds out to him – narcissi flower next to the vessel. On the far right, the lovers Smi-lax and Crocus recline. She is holding white bindweed, he has crocuses in his hair; the flowers in which they will live on. Behind them, pheasant's eye springs from the lethal wound of the hunter Adonis, the lover of Venus. Next to him stands Hyacinth (like a Greek statue) who, during a game of discus, was lethally struck by Apollo's discus on the forehead, from whence the hyacinths now burgeon. Outside this circle around Flora we find Ajax, a hero of the Trojan war. In anger, he committed suicide by hurling himself upon his sword after quarelling with Odysseus. A carnation is growing next to him. The transformation into flowers ensures the dying eternal rebirth. This is underlined by the presence of the herm of the god of fertility, Priapus, on the far left. The individual stories are found in Ovid, but their juxtaposition in Flora's garden seems to have been inspired by a poem by Giambattista Marino, one of Poussin's benefactors in Rome.

Claude Lorrain (Claude Gellée)

Chamagne near Mirecourt 1600-Rome 1682

Landscape with the Flight to Egypt
Signed lower left: CLAVDE IVEF ROMA 1647
Canvas, 102 x 134 cm
First mentioned in the inventory of 1754.
Gal. no. 730

Claude Gellée came from Lorraine, hence the name »Le Lorrain«. However, he lived and worked, from an early age, almost exclusively in Rome. His fame as a landscape artist was so great that his paintings were already being copied during his lifetime. In order to protect himself from such works, he made drawings of finished compositions in his *Liber veritatis* from 1635. The *Landscape with the Flight to Egypt* appears there as number 110. He sets the biblical theme in the dark wood on the far left. The countryside is bathed in a clear morning light. Our gaze is drawn to ancient buildings, a viaduct and a distant town. The atmosphere created by contrasting light and darkness, the balanced distribution of beautiful natural motifs and, last but not least, the idyll with the shepherds in the foreground, create the ideal landscape which is so typical of Claude Lorrain's work.

Salvator Rosa

Arenella near Naples 1615-Rome 1673

Woodland Scene with Three Philosophers
Signed below on stone with monogram SR
(ligated)
Canvas, 73 x 97.5 cm
First mentioned in the inventory of 1754.
Gal. no. 470

In contrast to Lorrain's classical landscapes, those of Salvator Rosa are wild and romantic in character, full of inhospitable mountains with rugged rocks, giant trees thwarting the storm, and gathering clouds. »If you have made yourself at home here, you are in the company of a great soul«, said Karoline Schlegel in front of the Dresden painting in 1799. The English romantics, in particular, were fascinated by Rosa's painting and his eccentric »soul«. Rosa was both a musician and poet, formed a group of actors with whom he produced satires (which made him many enemies), and was a follower of Stoic philosophy. In this painting, he reminds viewers of Diogenes who led a natural life and showed contempt for all material wealth (cf. Jacob Jordaens). He even threw his cup away when he saw a boy raising water to his mouth in his hand. Rosa portrayed this theme in a print in 1662 and used the figures for the landscape of the same date.

Carlo Cignani

Bologna 1628-Forlì 1719

Joseph and Potiphar's Wife
Canvas, octagonal, 99 x 99 cm
Acquired in 1749. Gal. no. 387

Cignani's style is greatly influenced by the painting of Correggio and Carracci, by grace and dignity, which he combined in his »nuova maniera«. After a stay in Rome from 1662-65, where he was also stimulated by the work of the dominant Carlo Maratta, he became the leading painter of the late 17th century in Bologna. This scene of an unsuccessful attempt at seduction (Genesis 39: 1-12) was painted around 1678/80. Half-naked and full of desire, Potiphar's wife embraces Joseph, her husband's slave, while he raises his arms to ward her off and turns to flee. Cignani created both figures according to the principle of the »rotondita« – of circling movement – in this small section of picture. The skilful use of light emphasizes the clear meaning of the gestures.

Carlo Dolci

Florence 1616-Florence 1686

St Cecilia
Canvas, 96.5 x 81 cm
Acquired in 1742. Gal. no. 509

This work by Carlo Dolci bears witness, in its purest form, to the intense sentiment and religious inspiration of the Late Baroque. Dolci's representations of devout saints, smoothly shaped in bright colours, aroused great admiration among his contemporaries. In this work of 1671, Dolci shows St Cecilia, the patron saint of music, at the organ. Although there is no mention of this in the legend, artists frequently chose this motif. The white lilies symbolize her virginity, but also attempt to explain her name »Cecilia« as »coeli lilia«, lily of heaven. Dolci is one of the latest famous representatives of Florentine painting which had spearheaded the development of European art in the Early Renaissance and peaked, once again, in Mannerism.

Giuseppe Bartolomeo Chiari

Rome 1654-Rome 1727

Adoration of the Magi
Signed lower left: IOSEPH CLARUS
PINGEBAT. ANNO MDCCXIV.
Canvas, 245 x 281 cm
First mentioned in the inventory of 1754.
Gal. no. 444

The influence of Maratta's decisive style is apparent in the *Adoration of the Magi* by his most faithful and successful pupil, Chiari. It was painted in 1714 for the Gallery of the Vice Chancellor of the Curia, Cardinal Pietro Ottoboni. The composition was inspired by a representation of the same theme by Maratta (handed down to us in an engraving by N. Dorigny). Chiari based the group of angels, on the left, on his master's *Death of Joseph* of 1676 (Kunsthistorisches Museum, Vienna). The painter also produced a smaller version (Staatliche Museen Berlin-Dahlem) in perpendicular form, resulting in a diagonal rather than M-shaped composition.

Carlo Maratta

Camerano (Marche) 1625-Rome 1713

Nativity
Canvas, 99 x 75 cm
Acquired in 1744. Gal. no. 436

Carlo Maratta was the leading religious painter in Rome in the second half of the 17th century. He had seven successive reigning popes as patrons. His work was modelled on Raphael, Carracci and Correggio, but his style was powerful Late Baroque Classicism. He painted the *Nativity* as a repetition, with very few changes, of part of a lunette fresco which had been made for the Church of San Isidoro in Rome in 1652. Light radiates from the Child, illuminates Mary's face, and is reflected on the angels' faces. Correggio's famous *Nativity*, also in the Dresden Gallery (Gal. no. 152), undoubtedly influenced Maratta, showing him the great intimacy of the motif. His special devotion to the Madonna, whom he portrays with humanity in a lyrical and solemn atmosphere, is proved impressively by the inscription on his tomb in S. Maria degli Angeli, but also by his nickname in his youth »Carluccio delle Madonne«.

Francesco Trevisani

Capodistria (Istria) 1656-Rome 1745

Virgin and Child with the Infant St John the Baptist
Signed lower left in book: F. T. 1708
Canvas, 99.5 x 74 cm
Acquired in 1734. Gal. no. 448

Maratta's successors seemed to adopt a more gentle, sensitive tone which led to a markedly classicistic Roman Rococo. While Trevisani remains true to Maratta in his monumental *Death of Joseph* (S. Ignazio, Rome), he translates his strict academic approach into highly refined painting with a porcelain-smooth surface and splendid radiance. Although he follows in the Roman tradition, the potential of the highly decorative art of Veronese survives in his blended shades of colour. Trevisani was the favourite artist in the circle around Cardinal Ottoboni who owned the most important collection of contemporary painting at that time. In 1709, the Cardinal sent Louis XIV a Madonna (Louvre, Paris) which is very similar to the Dresden *Virgin and Child with the Infant St John the Baptist* of 1708. Painting of this perfection was to develop through Batoni to the Neoclassicism of Anton Raphael Mengs.

▷

Francesco Solimena

Canale di Serino near Avellino (Campania) 1657-
Barra near Naples 1747

Virgin and Child with St Francis of Paola
Canvas, 97.5 x 98.5 cm
Acquired in 1745. Gal. no. 497

Solimena represents Late Baroque painting in Naples where the chiaroscuro technique, developed by Ribera, had been advanced by Mattia Preti and Luca Giordano. After Giordano's appointment as painter to the Spanish court in 1692, Solimena became the uncontested leading painter. From Naples, he influenced painting in Venice, Austria and Southern Germany. This canvas, believed to have been produced around 1703-05, displays, in typical contrasts of light and dark, the distinctly sculpted figures of the Madonna enthroned, St Francis of Paola on the right, and a guardian angel with a child in adoration on the left. On a pendant, Solimena portrays St Francis of Assisi reclining as he listens to an angel playing the violin (cf. painting by Guercino).

Giuseppe Maria Crespi, called Lo Spagnuolo

Bologna 1665-Bologna 1747

Confession
Canvas, 127 x 94.5 cm
Acquired in 1750. Gal. no. 396

The realistic, dramatic chiaroscuro technique from Naples appealed greatly to the Bolognese Crespi. According to the painter's son, this picture was inspired by a scene that Crespi had observed in a dark church where a beam of light illuminated the confessional to great effect. In the scene recreated in the artist's workshop, the viewer can almost hear the muffled mumblings of the woman in the confessional, on the left, and catches unawares the waiting sinner on the right, flicking through his list of sins. After painting this picture, Crespi was commissioned by Cardinal Ottoboni, in 1712, to paint scenes of the other six sacraments – baptism, confirmation, the Eucharist, matrimony, ordination and extreme unction – all of which are in Dresden. Thus, the Cardinal, who was also a patron of classicistic painting (Trevisani), received a series of sacred themes in a completely new, modestly realistic style. He must have been delighted by the contrast with the highly allegorical representations.

Giovanni Battista Piazzetta

Venice 1683-Venice 1754

Young Flag Bearer
Canvas, 87 x 71.5 cm
Acquired in 1743. Gal. no. 571

Although Piazzetta spent only a few years in Bologna, the painting of this city, and particularly the style of Crespi, provided the basis for his creative work. With dramatic compositions, concentrating on the contrast of shades of white and dark brown, he produced his own style of painting which was a major departure from the prevailing luminous Rococo painting of Sebastiano Ricci or the pastels of Rosalba Carriera. In his highly picturesque *Young Flag Bearer*, created around 1725/30, the content of an entire history painting is condensed into one figure, into a single motif. This prompted Jean Cocteau to say rightly: »This boy is a relative of the Gavroche at the barricades. Delacroix and Courbet would have found him a place in a scene of the Commune.«

Count Pietro Rotari

Verona 1707-St Petersburg 1762

Sleeping Girl
Canvas, 44 x 35 cm
Acquired in 1925. Gal. no. 600 B

Rotari spent several years in Venice before moving to Rome and Naples to continue his studies. He achieved his greatest fame with his genre-like portraits of girls, showing the entire spectrum between flirtatiousness and sentimentality. In 1757, after a stay in Dresden, Rotari went to St Petersburg as court painter to Empress Elisabeth. There he created hundreds of these paintings which still fill entire walls in Peterhof. Although the variety of gracefully inclined heads is amazing, the individual picture remains captivating, particularly when it is painted as fluently as this.

Giovanni Battista Tiepolo   ▷

Venice 1696-Madrid 1770

St Anne's Vision
Signed lower left on bridge pier:
Gio. Batta. Tiepolo. O. 1759
Canvas, 244 x 120 cm
Acquired in 1926. Gal. no. 580 A

Count Algarotti arranged for King August III and Count Brühl to purchase works by Tiepolo as early as 1744, but when they died the paintings were sold. The Gallery did not acquire works by Tiepolo again until a much later date. Baroque painting reached its zenith in his widely acclaimed works. Tiepolo's painting full of bright, airy colours can probably be stud-ied best in his frescoes (for example, in the Residence in Würzburg). Nevertheless, the Dresden canvases also reveal the character of his art. *St Anne's Vision* was painted, in 1759, for the Church of S. Chiara in Cividale (Friuli); town and church are represented in the lower left of the picture. It was only in her old age that St Anne gave birth to a daughter, Mary, who, in this picture, seems to be carried by angels. The girl's status as the future mother of Christ is emphasized by the presence of God the Father.

Sebastiano Ricci

Belluno 1659-Venice 1734

Sacrifice to Vesta
Canvas, 56.5 x 73 cm
Acquired in 1743. Gal. no. 549

Under the influence of the bright, festive frescoes of Cortona and Giordano, Ricci renewed Venetian painting in the spirit of Veronese, while the Genuese Magnasco inspired him to adopt a light, almost sketched style of painting. The *Sacrifice to Vesta* and its pendant, the *Sacrifice to Silenus*, are among Ricci's most brilliantly coloured, mature works. They were painted for Philippe Duc d'Orléans who died in 1723, shortly before they were completed. Vesta, the Roman goddess of hearth and household, was served by chastely clad virgin priestesses. The arrangement of the picture emphasizes that the figures offering sacrifices are subordinate to the Vestal Virgin. The pendant has a similar pyramidal composition, and the distribution of light and shadow is coordinated in the two paintings. The columns, temple and trees, like a theatre setting, show that Sebastiano Ricci was greatly influenced by Veronese.

Canaletto (Antonio Canal)

Venice 1697-Venice 1768

Grand Canal in Venice with the Rialto Bridge
Canvas, 146 x 234 cm
First mentioned in the inventory of 1754.
Gal. no. 581

In Venice, an individual style of vedute developed to record the special magic of the city with its fabulous canals and palaces, bridges and gondolas. Antonio Canal's work, which was greatly influenced, in Rome, by the Dutch painter Gaspar van Wittel, follows the topographical details very accurately, but is then filled with atmosphere. The light of the stormy clouded sky breaks in the rippling water in a multitude of colours, creating emerald-green depths, warm, sunny and cool shining surfaces. After 1730, his style became noticeably more schematic – otherwise he probably would not have been able to satisfy the enormous demand of his clients from all over the world. They visited Venice on their Grand Tour and were eager to have views of the »Queen of the Adriatic«.

Bernardo Bellotto, called Canaletto   ▷

Venice 1721-Warsaw 1780

Dresden from the Right Bank of the Elbe,
below the Augustus Bridge
Signed: Bernardo Bellotto detto Canaleto
F. anº. 1748
Canvas, 133 x 237 cm
First mentioned in the inventory of 1754.
Gal. no. 606

Understandably, the court of Dresden wanted the beauty of the flourishing city to be preserved for posterity in large vedute. Therefore, in 1747 Bellotto, a pupil of his uncle Antonio Canal, was called to the court on the river Elbe. There he painted his 25 impressive views of Dresden in its Baroque splendour. They are both first-class historical documents and major works of art. This characteristic skyline, seen from the right bank of the river Elbe, about on a level with the Japanese Palais,

became the »classic« view. It shows the famous Dresden bridge rebuilt by Matthäus Daniel Pöppelmann, the end of which forms the base of the Brühlsche Terrasse, named after Count Heinrich von Brühl. In the middle, the bridge seems to support the dome of the Frauenkirche (Church of Our Lady) by George Bähr, which had just been completed. In contrast, the tower of the Catholic Hofkirche (Court Church) was still under construction, so Bellotto painted it, with its scaffolding, after the building plans of Gaetano Chiaveri. In this painting, Bellotto emphasizes the Hofkirche, the high centre and side aisles of which are still two different colours. Behind the church we see the palace with its mighty tower, and further to the left the steeple of the old Kreuzkirche (Church of the Holy Cross).

Bernardo Bellotto, called Canaletto

Venice 1721-Warsaw 1780

The Zwinger in Dresden
Canvas, 134 x 237 cm
Delivered in 1753. Gal. no. 629

The Zwinger – a military word used to describe
the area between the palace and the fortifica-
tions – is one of the finest examples of German
Baroque architecture. It was commissioned by
August the Strong and built between 1710 and
1732. Matthäus Daniel Pöppelmann designed
it as open-air ceremonial grounds surrounded
by six pavilions connected by galleries. In Bellotto's day they were already used to house the
library and the art and natural history collections. This view is from the Wallpavillon
(Rampart Pavilion) to the Stadtpavillon (City
Pavilion) in the centre, with the Kreuzkirche
(Church of the Holy Cross) behind it to the
left, and the mighty roof of the Sophienkirche
(Church of St Sophie) to the right. The long
galleries on the right are dominated by the fine-
membered Kronentor (Crown Gate). In 1732
the opposite side was closed by a painted wall;
this is the site of Gottfried Semper's Paintings
Gallery, built from 1847 to 1855. Bellotto's
views are not simply architectural records.
They portray daily life on the market squares
and streets of Dresden; the comings and goings
of rich and poor. Bellotto's skilled perfection
is amazing. He achieves striking effects with
the simplest of means, shaping ornaments on
buildings, and figures, in a relief of light and
shadow, with just a few strokes and dots. With
precision and clarity, Bellotto shows us a past
world which has remained alive in his paintings.

Rosalba Carriera

Venice 1675-Venice 1757

Prince Frederick Christian of Saxony
Pastels on paper, 63.5 x 51.5 cm
Acquired in 1739. Gal. no. P 2

In the Rococo period, with its preference for
light and airy painting, pastels (dry pigments
bound with gum in stick form) became a popular means of artistic expression, particularly
for portraits. The Venetian Rosalba Carriera
was a source of great inspiration, her graceful
works being held in high esteem throughout
Europe. The Goncourt brothers said Rosalba's
portraits showed »A resemblance, as light as
a breath of air, with a fine glowing colour«.
However, she also knew how to combine the
delicacy of the drawing with the depth of
penetration of character studies. The portrait
of the young prince was produced in Venice
in 1739. The artist also made portraits of
numerous other members of the court. With
the 75 pastel drawings still in Dresden today,
the Gallery has the world's largest collection
of her works.

Antoine Watteau

Valenciennes 1684-Nogent-sur-Marne 1721

Outdoor Recreation
Canvas, 60 x 75 cm
First mentioned in the Guarienti inventory
(1747-1750).
Gal. no. 781

Watteau revered Rosalba Carriera; he even acquired one of her pastels in exchange for one of his own works. His enthusiasm is not surprising, since his paintings display a similarly bright and cheerful world, rejecting the »grand goût« of the art at the court of the Sun King. Everyday scenes, gallant adventures, chinoiserie and the theatre came into fashion. Watteau's »fêtes galantes« were probably inspired by Rubens' *Garden of Love*, and certainly by the theatre. Watteau's *Outdoor Recreation* is structured like a stage, with the apron for the actors at the front and the landscape as backdrop. In addition to this work, dated around 1720, the Dresden Gallery owns Watteau's *Banquet of Love*.

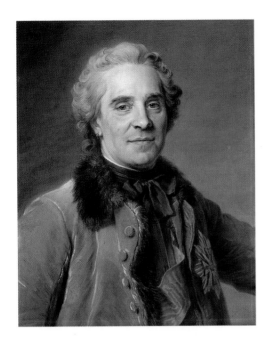

Maurice Quentin De La Tour

Saint-Quentin 1704-Saint-Quentin 1788

Count Moritz of Saxony, Marshal of France
Pastel on paper, 59.5 x 49 cm
First mentioned in the 1765 catalogue.
Gal. no. P 164

De La Tour's attention was drawn to the pastel technique by the appearance of Rosalba Carriera in Paris in 1719/20. From then on, he was to work exclusively in pastels. His delicately coloured portrait of Count Moritz of Saxony concentrates on the main features of the subject's character. The picture displays none of the grand gestures of the state portrait, found in the work of Rigaud and Largillierre. The count is not presented as a successful marshal whose victories in the Austrian War of Succession were decisive for France's position in the Peace of Aix-la-Chapelle of 1748, the year the portrait was made, but as an intellectual friend of Voltaire and the Marquise de Pompadour.

Jean-Etienne Liotard

Geneva 1702-Geneva 1789

Self-portrait
Pastel on paper, 60.5 x 46.5 cm
First mentioned in the 1765 catalogue.
Gal. no. P 159

Liotard was highly esteemed at many courts. His travels took him all over Europe, even as far as Constantinople in 1738-42. Shortly afterwards he created this *Self-portrait*. Unlike Rosalba Carriera's portraits, this is matter-of-fact and smoothly executed. He was not interested in making skin and materials shimmer and vibrate, but in an objective representation which is frozen in time. He also set great store by the use of local colour. This self-portrait shows that he liked to dress in »Turkish« costume, in keeping with the fashions of »Turquerie« and »Chinoiserie« which were often mixed together at that time.

Jean-Etienne Liotard

Geneva 1702-Geneva 1789

Chocolate Girl
Pastel on parchment, 82.5 x 52.5 cm
Acquired in 1745. Gal. no. P 161

Liotard produced his *Chocolate Girl* in Vienna and sold it, in 1745, to Count Francesco Algarotti in Venice. The latter's understanding of art is apparent from the lines he wrote about the pastel to his friend Pierre-Jean Mariette: »The work is almost without shadows, against a light-coloured ground, gaining its light from two windows reflected in the glass. It is worked in half-tones, with unnoticeable gradations of light, and of a perfect relief ... and although this work is European, it could be in the taste of the Chinese, the sworn enemies of the shadow, as you know. As to the work's perfection, it is a Holbein in pastels.« In another letter he tells Count Brühl that Rosalba Carriera and all Venetian painters thought the *Chocolate Girl* was »the most beautiful pastel ever seen«.

Jan van Eyck

Probably Maaseyck near Maastricht c. 1390-
Bruges 1441

Winged Altarpiece
Signed in concave moulding of frame of centre
panel: Johannes de Eyck me fecit et có[m]plevit
Anno Domini MCCCCXXXVII. Als ixh xan.
Oak, centre panel 33.1 x 27.5,
each wing 33.1 x 13.6 cm (measured with
the original frame)
First mentioned in the inventory of 1754.
Gal. no. 799

»Jan van Eyck produced and completed me in
the year of the Lord 1437. As well as I [Van
Eyck] am able«, is the English translation of
the signature on the original frame which also
provides Latin texts on the holy scenes: In
the centre the Virgin and Child, on the left
Archangel Michael recommending a donor,
and on the right St Catharine. The exterior
shows the Annunciation to Mary by the
Archangel Gabriel, in grisaille; the figures are
like statuettes in niches. The donor has not yet
been identified. A coat of arms at the top right
could indicate the Genoese Giustiniani family.
This small altar for private prayer concentrates
on Mary and the Christ Child who, on his
banderole (text from Matthew 11: 29), exhorts
the donor to follow him. The complicated programmatic content of the ornamental sculpture, the formal means of perspective and, last
but not least, the brilliant painting in splendid
colours make this altar a veritable jewel of
Netherlandish painting. It is easy to see why
Jan van Eyck was the most important artist of
his day, and was soon to be called the inventor of oil painting.

Joos van Cleve (Joos van der Beke)

Cleves c. 1480/85-Antwerp 1540

(Small) Adoration of the Magi
Oak, 110 x 70.5 cm
First mentioned in the 1812 catalogue. Gal. no. 809

The Dresden Gallery has a second »Adoration of the Magi« by van Cleve; it is twice as high and dated around 1525, more than ten years earlier than this smaller version. Both paintings display a delight in telling the story of the three kings who travel many miles, with their caravans, to make their bizarre and costly appearance before the Christ Child in the ruins of a heathen temple. The eldest king has already fallen to his knees, while the second, wearing a Phrygian cap, and the youngest, a Moor, approach. According to tradition, the Child is worshipped by all mankind: the three parts of the known world at that time – Europe, Asia and Africa – and the three ages of man. Joos van Cleve, who represented himself in the middle ground of both paintings, thus links Late Gothic tradition with Renaissance motifs. This is typical of Antwerp Mannerism after 1510.

Herri met de Bles

Bouvignes-les-Dinant c. 1510-probably Antwerp after 1555

Monkeys Steal the Goods of a Grocer Sleeping under a Tree
Oak, 59.5 x 85.5 cm
First mentioned in the inventory of 1722-1728. Gal. no. 806

The artist, who was influenced by Joachim Patinir, was among the first to specialize in landscapes. During a stay in Italy he was given the nickname »Civetta« after the owl that frequently appears in his pictures (here, on the left in the tree). However, this is not a signature. The landscape became a theme for pictorial treatment at the same time as profane storytelling in pictures. Here a hoard of monkeys steals all the grocer's goods while he is asleep. Karel van Mander, who describes the picture in 1604, says one interpretation is mockery of the pope, but the theme was already widespread in Italy and Flanders in the 15th century. The 1562 engraving, after Pieter Bruegel, is best-known.

Maerten I van Valckenborch

Louvain 1535-Frankfurt am Main 1612

The Building of the Tower of Babel
Signed lower centre: MARTIN VAN VALCKEN-
BORCH FECIT ET INVENTOR MVV 1595
Oak, 75.5 x 105 cm
Acquired in 1699. Gal. no. 832

The strong impulse that Pieter Bruegel's art
gave to Netherlandish painting is evident from
the many representations of the building of the
tower of Babel. They are nearly all based on
Bruegel's 1563 formulation of the theme
(Kunsthistorisches Museum, Vienna). This
painting by Maerten van Valckenborch is no
exception. It shows the mighty building which
was to reach heaven. However, God punished
the people and King Nimrod for such pre-
sumptuousness by »confounding« their language. They had to stop building because they
could not understand one another (Genesis
11: 1-9).

Jan Brueghel the Elder

Brussels 1568-Antwerp 1625

*Coastal Landscape with the Calling
of Peter and Andrew*
Signed lower right: BRVEGHEL 1608
Copper, 50 x 66 cm
First mentioned in the inventory of 1722-1728.
Gal. no. 883

Pieter Bruegel's youngest son specialized in ex-
quisitely executed still-lifes of flowers and
landscapes in radiant colours. His landscapes,
with the traditional division of the grounds
into blue depths, with green and brown surfaces in front of them, are brought alive by brilliantly painted, colourful figures. Such masterpieces decorated the Kunstkammer of the
connoisseurs. They must have taken pleasure
not only in the overall impression but also in
the minute detail, otherwise they would not
have noticed the small biblical scene at the centre of the picture.

Joos de Momper

Antwerp 1564-Antwerp 1635

Town in the Valley
Remains of signature lower left: M...
Oak, 83 x 125 cm
Acquired in 1875. Gal. no. 874

De Momper's compositions frequently resemble those of Jan Brueghel who occasionally painted the figures for him, as was the case in this picture. Nevertheless, Joos de Momper developed his own characteristic sketchy technique with a dynamic brush language of numerous small hooks and strokes. Thus he was able to produce large numbers of monumental landscapes and very decorative friezes and series. His painting stands midway between the detailed works of Jan Brueghel the Elder and the grandiose landscapes of Peter Paul Rubens.

Peter Paul Rubens

Siegen 1577-Antwerp 1640

Wild Boar Hunt
Oak, 137 x 168 cm
Acquired in 1749. Gal. no. 962

The Dresden Gallery owns a number of works by the greatest Flemish Baroque painter, Peter Paul Rubens. With his large workshop, numerous employees and pupils, he was able to fill vast orders for churches and royal houses. Rubens was extremely well-educated, ennobled several times, and employed for diplomatic services. His great imagination enabled him to formulate complicated themes in new ways. This is demonstrated by the immensely dynamic *Wild Boar Hunt*, painted around 1615/20, at the beginning of his interest in landscapes. Even the trees twist and turn when they hear the barking of the dogs as they corner the wild boar at the centre of the picture.

Peter Paul Rubens

Siegen 1577-Antwerp 1640

Diana's Return from the Hunt
Canvas, 136 x 184 cm
Acquired in 1709. Gal. no. 962 A

Diana, the goddess of hunting and virginity, and three of her companions encounter a group of satyrs who, with their fruit, represent earthly lustfulness. Viewers are curious about the outcome of the bold offer of the satyr in the centre who, with his bacchic bunches of grapes, would like to step over the boundary between the two groups. Both the theme and Rubens' painting are sensuous. In this work dated around 1616, Rubens let Frans Snyders paint the fruit and animals.

Peter Paul Rubens   ▷

Siegen 1577-Antwerp 1640

Bathsheba at the Fountain
Oak, 175 x 126 cm
Acquired in 1749. Gal. no. 965

One evening, from the roof of his palace, King David »saw a woman washing herself; and the woman was very beautiful to look upon ... And David sent messengers, and took her; and she came in unto him, and he lay with her«. Rubens combines these two scenes from the Old Testament (2 Samuel 11: 2-4). At the upper left we see the king, while a black page brings the message in a letter. Rubens was inspired by the beauty of Hélène Fourment, his second young wife, for this delicately painted late work of around 1635.

Frans Snyders

Antwerp 1579-Antwerp 1657

Still-life with Bitch and Litter, and Two Cooks
Canvas, 197 x 325 cm
Acquired in 1743. Gal. no. 1195

Frans Snyders' large hunting and kitchen still-lifes, brimful of objects, were undoubtedly influenced by Rubens' dynamic compositions and magnificent colours. His still-lifes are rarely »still«. At the lower right, a bitch with five puppies growls at an intruder, at the top two doves are cooing, and under the table a cat is keeping watch. In the 16th century, in pictures by Aertsen and Beuckelaer, such displays of excess had been confronted with biblical scenes urging the viewer to renounce worldly pleasures. Here we see the festive world of the Flemish Baroque; the titilation of the senses. The two figures were added to the still-life by Rubens, for whom Synders frequently painted animals and fruit.

Jan Wildens

Antwerp 1586-Antwerp 1653

Winter Landscape with Hunter
Signed lower left: IAN.WILDENS FECIT 1624
Canvas, 194 x 292 cm
First mentioned in the inventory of 1722-1728.
Gal. no. 1133

In Rubens' workshop, Jan Wildens was frequently responsible for the landscape backgrounds in large compositions with figures. In contrast, the Dresden winter landscape is one of Wildens' own works. He used another artist's composition as a model only for the greyhound on the left. Rubens also used this figure on several occasions. The close range of the landscape is unusual, with the hunter and large group of bare trees dominating the foreground, and the background suggested only by the icy colours. Most Dutch winter landscapes show wide open spaces, populated by numerous small figures (cf. Jan van Goyen).

Anthony van Dyck

Antwerp 1599-London 1641

St Jerome
Canvas, 195 x 215 cm
First mentioned in the Guarienti inventory
(1747-1750).
Gal. no. 1024

Anthony van Dyck was the most outstanding painter in Rubens' workshop from 1616/18 to 1620. Previously, as a precocious child wonder, he is said to have had his own workshop with assistants. *St Jerome* dates from his time with Rubens who later owned the picture. Van Dyck's preoccupation with the art of the older master can be studied excellently in Dresden because the Gallery also owns a slightly earlier *St Jerome* by Rubens. Despite the similarities of form and content, Rubens' saint looks calm, while Van Dyck's seems more excited. According to the legend, the cardinal and church elder Jerome had gone out into the wilderness to do penance. He is often shown with a lion which never left his side after he had removed a thorn from its paw.

Anthony van Dyck

Antwerp 1599-London 1641

*Portrait of a Man in Armour with
a Red Arm Band*
Canvas, 90 x 70 cm
Acquired in 1741. Gal. no. 1026

Van Dyck achieved fame primarily as a portraitist. Way beyond Antwerp, during his stay in Italy from 1621 to 1627 and, in particular, at the English court from 1632, he created portrait forms that were to serve as models for centuries to come. This portrait of a soldier, produced around 1625-27, probably was not painted as an individual, but as an heroic figure. Ideal portraits of Roman emperors, for example by Titian, may have played an influential role.

Adriaen Brouwer

Oudenaarde 1605/06-Antwerp 1638

A Father's Unpleasant Duties
Oak, 20 x 13 cm
First mentioned in the 1817 catalogue.
Gal. no. 1057

Before David Teniers the Younger, Brouwer was the most famous Flemish genre painter of the 17th century. His pictures of peasants smoking and drinking, of card games and brawls, show dramatically both human passions and vices. They caricature uncouth and base instincts which undoubtedly amused the collectors of his pictures, including Rubens. Brouwer's painting of *A Father's Unpleasant Duties* fulfils this very purpose. It also symbolizes »smell«, as it is often represented in series of the five senses.

Jacob Jordaens

Antwerp 1593-Antwerp 1678

Diogenes with a Lantern in Search of a Man at the Market
Canvas, 233 x 349 cm
Acquired in 1742. Gal. no. 1010

After Rubens' death in 1640, Jordaens received the most orders for large paintings in public and private buildings in the Netherlands. Next to the works of Rubens and Van Dyck, his figures look coarse and exaggerated. However, this style is ideal for characterizing man in this way. Jordaens' large painting of 1642 shows the Greek philosopher Diogenes at the market, in broad daylight, with a burning lantern. When asked what he was doing, he said he was looking for a »Man«. Diogenes was the best-known representative of cynicism. He showed contempt for all excesses of wealth and enjoyment, accepting only man's most elementary needs. As viewers, we may be amused by the stout people at the market shaking with laughter at Diogenes, but we cannot help feeling that, at any moment, the philosopher will step out of the canvas in search of the real »Man« among us.

David Teniers the Younger

Antwerp 1610-Brussels 1690

Temptation of St Anthony in the Grotto
Signed lower right: D. TENIERS. F.
Copper, 69 x 86 cm
First mentioned in the inventory of 1722-28.
Gal. no. 1079

His great productivity, versatility and, ultimately, his ascent to court painter and director of the gallery of the governor, Leopold Wilhelm, in Brussels, made Teniers one of the most successful artists of his day. His works were still copied enthusiastically in the 18th century and sought by royal collectors. His best-known works are peasant scenes, which are friendlier than Brouwer's, but he also painted other themes, such as the *Temptation of St Anthony*. The Dresden picture of about 1645 shows the hermit being exposed to all kinds of devilry during his prayers. A procuress draws his attention to a tempting beauty whose claw-feet are also the work of the devil. The humorously painted picture shows the saint a second time, in the background, as he visits the hermit Paul. Each day a raven brings Paul half a piece of bread; it brings him a whole piece during Anthony's visit.

Jan Davidsz de Heem

Utrecht 1606-Antwerp 1683/84

Still-life with Bird's Nest
Signed lower right: J. D. De Heem fecit
Canvas, 89 x 72 cm
Acquired in 1709. Gal. no. 1261

De Heem introduced many new ideas to still-life painting. He combined the Dutch attention to detail with the Flemish love for displays of splendour, thus developing different types of picture, such as still-lifes of sumptuously laid tables or – as in this case – corners full of decay. These arrangements are truly extraordinary. A variety of fruit has been placed inside a ruin teeming with animals. Every nook and cranny is inhabited by tiny creatures painted with incredible perfection. The viewer is not only fascinated by the numbers of creatures crawling and flying across the canvas, but reminded of the cycle of growth and decline in nature.

Jan Davidsz de Heem

Utrecht 1606-Antwerp 1683/84

Memento Mori! Flowers with Skull
Signed on note on right: Memento Mori J.D. De Heem
Canvas, 87.5 x 65 cm
First mentioned in the inventory of 1722-1728.
Gal. no. 1265

De Heem's mastery is apparent in every detail of this still-life, showing a decorative arrangement of brightly coloured blooms in all their splendour. However, the painter reminds us, in a clear message, of the death of all natural things: He wrote »Memento Mori« on the note which is held in place by a large shiny snail shell. A closer look reveals a skull crowned with ivy in the background. This reminder of death should encourage the viewer to lead a life which is worthy of the glories of the hereafter. The ivy, an evergreen, underlines this idea, being a symbol of hope and eternal life. Similarly, the striking ears of wheat among the flowers stand for the Resurrection.

David Teniers the Younger

Antwerp 1610-Brussels 1690

Nicolaes van Veerendael

Antwerp 1640-Antwerp 1691

Carstian Luyckx

Antwerp 1623-after 1670

In Front of the Kitchen
Signed lower right: D. T.; upper left:
N. V. Verendael f;
centre: Carstian Luckx
Canvas, 83 x 120 cm
Acquired in 1723. Gal. no. 1091

Each of the three artists signed part of this joint work: Teniers his characteristic kitchen scene on the right, Veerendael the bunch of flowers on the left and Luyckx the still-life below, comprising dead birds, a decoy box, fish and a cat. The painting, dated around 1672, is reminiscent of representations of the four elements, the flowers symbolizing earth, the kitchen range fire, the fish water and the birds air. Joint works of this kind were not unusual since many painters were highly specialized at that time. In this case, a collector could boast of having the highlights of three artists on a single painting.

Cornelis Cornelisz van Haarlem

Haarlem 1562-Haarlem 1638

Venus, Bacchus and Ceres
Signed lower left: CH. 1614
Canvas, 154 x 184 cm
Acquired in 1723. Gal. no. 851

Cornelis van Haarlem belonged to the generation of Dutch Mannerists whose style was influenced decisively by Bartholomäus Spranger in Prague and interpretations of his art by Karel van Mander and Hendrik Goltzius. In 1584 Cornelis joined the latter two artists to establish a kind of academy in Haarlem. The theme of his painting of 1614 was extremely popular in this group. It shows Venus with Amor, as goddess of love on the left, Bacchus, the god of wine in the centre, and Ceres, the goddess of the fruits of the field with ears of wheat in her hair. The painting illustrates a verse by Terence (The Eunuch 732), according to which Venus would freeze without Ceres and Bacchus. In other words, love grows cold without food and drink.

Gerard van Honthorst

Utrecht 1590-Utrecht 1656

The Dentist
Signed centre right: G. v: Hont Horst: fe. 1622
Canvas, 147 x 219 cm
Acquired in 1749. Gal. no. 1251

Apart from Hendrick ter Brugghen, Honthorst is considered the most important of the Utrecht Caravaggisti. In 1610, he went to Rome where he stayed for more than ten years and was called »Gherardo delle Notti« – Gerard of the Nights – because of his painting. He integrated the new chiaroscuro painting of Michelangelo Merisi, called Caravaggio, into his night scenes with artificial sources of light. With rough, striking figures in the foreground, he creates a realism that contrasts strongly with the paintings of the previous Mannerist generation. In this picture, a single candle illuminates the entire group of inquisitive onlookers crowded around the dentist and his poor patient. As in earlier representations (for example, by Lucas van Leyden, copper engraving 1523), this lust for sensation is punished immediately: On the far left, a pickpocket helps himself to a purse.

Rembrandt (Rembrandt Harmensz van Rijn)

Leiden 1606-Amsterdam 1669

Rembrandt and Saskia in the Parable
of the Prodigal Son
Remains of signature centre left: Rembrandt f.
Canvas, 161 x 131 cm
Acquired in 1751. Gal. no. 1559

The Dresden Gallery has one of the richest collections of paintings by Rembrandt and his pupils. This self-portrait with Saskia of about 1635 is among the best-known, and is frequently quoted as anecdotal evidence of Rembrandt's happiest period. He originally planned the composition as a horizontal representation of the parable of the Prodigal Son (St Luke 15: 11-32), but then he made two very radical changes. He cut the picture on the left and painted over a lute player in the centre, thereby turning the picture into a double portrait. We can only speculate about the reasons for these changes. Rembrandt was influenced, inter alia, by the Utrecht Caravaggisti, particularly by Hendrick ter Brugghen. They painted drinking scenes of similar composition.

Rembrandt (Rembrandt Harmensz van Rijn)

Leiden 1606-Amsterdam 1669

Rape of Ganymede
Signed and dated on drapery: Rembrandt. fe 1635
Canvas, 177 x 130 cm
Acquired in 1751. Gal. no. 1558

According to the Greek myth, Ganymede had grown into such a beautiful boy that the gods wanted him to become Zeus' cupbearer. However, Zeus felt so erotically attracted to the youth that he took the form of an eagle and carried him up to heaven. Ganymede was later immortalised as the constellation Aquarius. Rembrandt's realistic picture shows a writhing, screaming child who passes water out of fear as the eagle seizes him roughly by the drapery. According to Karel van Manders' interpretation of the myth of 1604, Ganymede may be seen as the sign of the zodiac that brings rain. However, he could also symbolize a child that dies young with a pure soul, as seen in the peaceful paintings of the same theme by Rembrandt's pupil Nicolaes Maes. Whatever the case, it is easy to understand why Rembrandt was soon condemned as a »heretic« because of his realism. He painted »Venus like a washerwoman or peat cutter« and said his work was a true »imitation of nature, everything else (is) empty ornamentation« (Andries Pels, 1681).

Rembrandt (Rembrandt Harmensz van Rijn)

Leiden 1606-Amsterdam 1669

Samson Proposing the Riddle at the Wedding Feast
Signed lower centre: Rembrandt. f. 1638
Canvas, 126 x 175 cm
First mentioned in the inventory of 1722-1728. Gal. no. 1560

Samson, the Old Testament hero renowned for his strength, proposed the following riddle at his wedding feast: »Out of the eater came forth meat, and out of the strong came forth sweetness.« None of the guests from the tribe of the Philistines, who ruled Israel, knew the solution, but the young bride enticed Samson to tell her the answer which she then passed on to her people. When they said: »What is sweeter than honey? and what is stronger than a lion?« Samson realized that they knew about the lion he had killed and the swarm of bees in its carcass (Judges 14: 10-18). Rembrandt portrays the scene magnificently. It is full of amusing details, and unsurpassed in the theatrical contrast between a man who thinks he is wiser than everyone else, and his wife who is waiting confidently for her moment of triumph. Rembrandt's importance as a storyteller was extolled by Philips Angel in 1641 when he described this picture in his »Lof der Schilder-Konst« (In Praise of the Art of Painting).

Ferdinand Bol

Dordrecht 1616-Amsterdam 1680

The Dream of Jacob's Ladder
Signed lower right: f. Bol fecit
Canvas, 128 x 97 cm
First mentioned in the inventory of 1722-1728.
Gal. no. 1604

Bol was Rembrandt's pupil in the 1630s, as is evident fromt his early paintings of biblical scenes. These include *The Dream of Jacob's Ladder* (Genesis 28: 11-15) of 1642. Its structure and details are similar to those of a painting of the same subject, and of about the same period, by another Rembrandt pupil, Gerbrand van den Eeckhout (National Museum, Warsaw). The Dresden Gallery also has a much later version (1669) of the same subject by Eeckhout (Gal. no. 1618 A). The theme, the strange meeting of an angel with a human being, was certainly inspired by Rembrandt. Other pupils' works deal with similar situations with biblical figures, such as Hagar, Daniel, Tobias or Gideon (also painted by Bol and Eeckhout in 1641/42). From 1650 Bol increasingly turned away from Rembrandt's style and then, as a rich burgher, around 1669, he gave up painting altogether.

Jan Victors

Amsterdam 1619-Eastern India after 1676

The Finding of Moses
Signed lower left: Jan Victors fe. 1653
Canvas, 160 x 199 cm
First mentioned in the 1835 catalogue.
Gal. no. 1615

Jan Victors must have visited Rembrandt's workshop in the second half of the 1630s. As a strict Calvinist, he was prohibited from painting God. Therefore, he chose his biblical themes exclusively from the Old Testament and avoided representations of God the Father or Christ. In Exodus 2: 2-9, we read that a woman left her three-month-old son Moses in the bulrushes because she wanted to save his life. The Pharoah had ordered that all the children of the Israelites, born in Egypt, be killed. When the Pharaoh's daughter finds Moses, she takes the advice of a servant girl and hands him over to a Hebrew nurse, without knowing that she has spoken to the foundling's sister and mother. This picture of great soulfulness has a counterpart (Gal. no. 1616) in Victors' *Finding of the Cup in Benjamin's Sack* (Genesis 44: 12). Here again, the Bible tells a story which ultimately leads to the saving of the Israelites in Egypt.

Aert de Gelder

Dordrecht 1645-Dordrecht 1727

Ecce Homo
Signed: A d Gelder. f. 1671
Canvas, 152 x 191 cm
Acquired in 1743. Gal. no. 1791

Aert de Gelder continued the style of his teacher Rembrandt until well after 1700. This *Ecce Homo* was painted two years after Rembrandt's death under the influence of his print, on the same theme, of 1656 (B. 76), although other prints by Rembrandt provided models for the individual figures. Aert de Gelder is also a storyteller. This picture includes a large number of exotically and imaginatively dressed actors and spectators, some of whom are hardly affected by what is happening.

Aert de Gelder

Dordrecht 1645-Dordrecht 1727

Man with Partisan
Canvas, 82.5 x 70.5 cm
Acquired in 1727. Gal. no. 1792

Aert de Gelder shows his esteem for his teacher in his *Self-portrait with* (Rembrandt's) *Hundred Guilder Print* (Hermitage, St Petersburg). In the Dresden picture, he turns to a motif from Rembrandt's *Night Watch* (Rijksmuseum, Amsterdam) which had commanded the admiration of contemporaries: The lance which Lieutenant Willem van Ruytenburch is holding looks as if it is about to pierce through the picture. Considering Aert de Gelder's reasons for painting the above-mentioned self-portrait, the man demonstrating Rembrandt's famous lance effect in this picture is thought to be the artist.

Gerard Dou ▷

Leiden 1613-Leiden 1675

The Painter in his Workshop
Signed half-left on table: G Dov 1647
Oak, 43 x 34.5 cm
First mentioned in the inventory of 1722-1728.
Gal. no. 1704

With great patience and diligence, Rembrandt's first pupil in Leiden developed a highly perfected style of painting which was to start an entire school of fine painters in Leiden. The brushwork is almost invisible on this self-portrait which, with its many attributes, is more like a self-declaration. The artist, drawing in his studio, is familiar with the laws of the visible world (globe), the right harmonies and proportions (music and musical instruments), the legacy of the mythology and art of Antiquity (sculptures). His painting can depict light, reflections, materials, even other forms of art, such as sculpture, and his drawing skills are used in other sciences – a universal claim of the »Hooge Schoole der Schilder-Konst« (The Art of Painting).

Caesar Boëtius van Everdingen

Alkmaar c. 1617-Alkmaar 1678

Bacchus with Two Nymphs and Amor
Signed lower left with monogram: CVE
Canvas, 147 x 161 cm
Acquired in 1865. Gal. no. 1834

Outside the Rembrandt School, the Haarlem Classicists produced large history paintings. Many of them were created for public buildings, and praised statesmanlike virtues or honourable judges of Antiquity. Van Everdingen, who had learnt with one of the Utrecht Caravaggisti, worked in Haarlem for a while until 1657. He developed his own style with idealized figures and light-coloured smooth painting. The reflections of light in the shadows make his figures look as if they are bathed in light. The Dresden picture of around 1650-60 is thought to portray Bacchus and Ariadne on Naxos. Its perspective suggests that it was painted as a fireplace piece.

Jan Vermeer

Delft 1632-Delft 1675

The Procuress
Signed lower right: J V Meer. 1656
Canvas, 143 x 130 cm
Acquired in 1741. Gal. no. 1335

Vermeer's early work carries on directly from the art of the Utrecht Caravaggisti of 1620-30 and their successors. As A. Mayer-Meintschel showed in 1986, this particular picture is influenced by a representation of the five senses by the Delft painter Christiaen van Couwenbergh. Vermeer places his life-sized half-figures behind a balustrade which is covered by a coat and a carpet. The latter is a mixture of patterns in the different shades of red and yellow used for the main characters, the customer and prostitute. The yellow is most intense around the man's hand on the girl's bosom. However, the centre of the picture is the act of payment, without which the man would not be able to make this gesture to the satisfaction of the old procuress next to him. The young man on the left, whose look draws us into the scene (and thus demands our comment), is thought to be the artist.

Jan Vermeer

Delft 1632-Delft 1675

Girl at a Window Reading a Letter
Illegible traces of signature centre right
Canvas, 83 x 64.5 cm
Acquired in 1742. Gal. no. 1336

This painting is one of Vermeer's early »still-life-like« representations with figures who are reading, writing, music-making, or engrossed in some other occupation. Vermeer had originally included a painting of Cupid on the wall behind the girl, using the picture language of his day to indicate that she is reading a love-letter. The curtain, painted later, also conceals glasses in the lower corner. In those days, paintings had curtains to protect them against the light and dust. Vermeer paints his curtain »in front of« his picture thus concealing the experimental nature of his composition: A high room with a small figure surrounded by furnishings which are only partly visible. The impression of chance conveyed by such an unusual and yet harmoniously balanced composition increases the illusionism of his painting. Vermeer emphasizes this with an almost three-dimensional painting technique with pastose colours, for example on the illuminated folds of the curtain.

The themes of letter-writing and letter-reading were represented primarily by fine painters, such as Gerard Dou or Frans van Mieris. Gerard ter Borch, who visited Vermeer in Delft in 1653, was particularly good at finding new motifs (see Gal. no. 1829, 1833). On this picture by his pupil Caspar Netscher, a young man is gazing into space as he looks for the right words. He could refer to the contemporary manuals on the art of writing. The most popular was *Le Secrétaire à la Mode* by Jean Puget de la Serre, 1643, which was also widely available in Holland, in numerous editions, for example in a Dutch translation of 1651. It provides examples of love-letters in selective but not exaggerated language. It is no wonder that some pictures of letter-writers have pendants in the form of letter-readers.

Caspar Netscher

Heidelberg (?) c. 1649-The Hague 1684

Man Writing a Letter
Signed on map on wall:
C Netscher. Fecit. 1665
Oak, rounded top, 27 x 18.5 cm
First mentioned in the inventory of 1722-1728.
Gal. no. 1346

Gabriel Metsu

Leiden 1629-Amsterdam 1667

Portrait of the Artist with his Wife
Isabella de Wolff in a Tavern
Signed upper left: G Metsú 1661
Oak, 35.5 x 30.5 cm
First mentioned in the inventory of 1722-1728
Gal. no. 1732

Metsu's picture of an affluent couple is fine painting at its best. There is no real evidence to support the anecdote that this is a portrait of the artist with his wife. However, their excesses at the tavern pose a threat both to their riches and morals. On the left, a maid records, on a board, how much has been consumed. Judging by the way the man is behaving, the total will rise. As in Rembrandt's *Self-portrait with Saskia* (Gal. no. 1559), the painter warns of the dangers of worldly excesses, analogously to the biblical parable of the Prodigal Son.

Adriaen van der Werff

Kralingen 1659-Rotterdam 1722

Pastoral Scene
Signed lower right: adr^n van der werff fec. an. 1689
Oak, 58.5 x 47.5 cm
Acquired in 1710. Gal. no. 1812

During his lifetime, »Ritter van der Werff« was celebrated like no other artist. Later he was criticised just as passionately. His formerly praised technical perfection was rejected as cold porcelain-like smoothness. Van der Werff perfected the techniques he had learnt from the fine painters of Leiden, translating their representations of everyday scenes into court language. His shepherdess is wearing expensive satins, his shepherd has settled next to a fountain with costly sculptures of putti, and on the right, half in the shade, we see the sculpture of Antiquity of the so-called *Dancing Faun* which Van der Werff painted after a print by Jan de Bisschop. Van der Werff's excellent painting technique emphasizes the scene's sensuousness, for he can reproduce all materials from rustling oak leaves to a delicate skin. This painting came to the Court of Dresden from Düsseldorf in 1710. It was a gift from the Elector of the Palatinate.

Nicolaes Pietersz Berchem

Haarlem 1620-Amsterdam 1683

A Merchant Receiving a Moor
at the Harbour Palace
Signed lower left: C Berchem f.
Transferred from wood to canvas, 94 x 98.5 cm
Acquired in 1727. Gal. no. 1479

Berchem is renowned primarily for his Italian-style landscapes with shepherds and animals, but around 1665 he also created several paintings with figures, demonstrating extremely fine skill. He delighted in all things foreign and exotic, and therefore placed his figures in southern palace architectures and harbours, as Jan Baptist Weenix had done. In this painting, Berchem plays uniquely with Mediterranean rays of light, making the warm colours glow. Since two similar pictures in the Geneva Museum illustrate biblical themes, this painting has been interpreted, inter alia, as »Pharaoh's proposal to Sarah« (Genesis 12: 18-20).

Pieter Claesz

Burgsteinfurt/Westphalia 1597/98-Haarlem 1661

Still-life with Silver-Gilt Cup
Monogram lower left: PC (linked)
Aº 1624
Oak, 65 x 55.5 cm
Acquired in 1875. Gal. no. 1370

Pieter Claesz became famous for his monochrome still-lifes of small meals, which he developed in Haarlem from the 1620s. These modest Dutch paintings contrast sharply with the exuberant, colourful Flemish still-lifes. This *Still-life with Silver-gilt Cup* was painted in 1624, at the beginning of the artist's career. At that time, the polished nautilus and other shells in the picture were extremely costly articles. Carnations, in bud and in full bloom, are lying on the table, while in the background, on the left, a young couple symbolizes the prime of life, in accordance with the picture tradition of the garden of love. However, all these items are transitory, like the time on the pocket watch; a message underlined by the skull on the far right.

Joseph de Bray

Haarlem, date of birth unknown-Haarlem 1664

Still-life with Poem in Praise of the Herring
Signed lower centre: Joh Bray. 1656
Oak, 57 x 48.5 cm
Acquired in 1741. Gal. no. 1407

This picture, with its explanatory text, is an exceptional example of Dutch still-life painting. De Bray depicts a poem, on the stone cartouche, which his uncle Jakob Westerbaen had translated freely from Latin. That text »Halecis salsati vires« was on a panel in the Theatrum Anatomicum of the medical faculty of the University of Leiden. Both the Latin text and Westerbaen's translation praise entertainingly the merits of the pickled herring: As a simple dish, it stimulates both the appetite and the digestion, and is far better able to promote a feeling of well-being than expensive medicines or succulent tidbits. In his still-life, the artist illustrates the ingredients mentioned in the text, thus emphasizing the praise of the pickled herring more forcibly than the Leiden panel. The Suermondt-Ludwig-Museum in Aachen has a more complex version.

Melchior de Hondecoeter

Utrecht 1636-Amsterdam 1695

Bird Concert
Canvas, 164 x 214 cm
First mentioned in the inventory of 1722-1728.
Gal. no. 1305

Hondecoeter ist *the* genre painter for farm-yard fowl and other birds which are usually depicted, in all their colourful splendour, in aristocratic parks. His rich repertoire of in-digenous and exotic birds is shown, in diffe-rent combinations, in large paintings. These also demonstrate Hondecoeter's interest in the diversity of nature, bucolic life and amusing decoration. He often gives his bird collections a setting of ancient fables or proverbs. Here we can read, on the score two birds are holding in their beaks, »Elck Voogel zingt, gelijk hij gebect is« – each bird sings in its own way, depending on the shape of its beak. It is not difficult to imagine what the concert sounds like under the direction of the foolish owl!

Jan van Goyen

Leiden 1596-The Hague 1656

Winter on the River
Signed lower right on boat: VGOYEN 1643
Oak, 68 x 90.5 cm
First mentioned in the 1812 catalogue.
Gal. no. 1338 B

Jan van Goyen was certainly Holland's most productive landscape painter. He also had a large number of pupils and followers. Towards the end of the 1620s, he developed the tonal landscape in which he reduced the colours to shades of grey and ochre. This restriction also resulted in a substantial increase in intermediate shades, permitting a new kind of painting of light and air, of haziness and changing weather conditions. Van Goyen's winter landscapes demonstrate clearly this achievement.

Philips Koninck

Amsterdam 1619-Amsterdam 1688

Dutch Landscape with View from the Dunes onto the Plane
Canvas, 122 x 165 cm
Acquired in 1905. Gal. no. 1612 A

The themes of Koninck's paintings are the broad expanse of the Dutch landscape, the constant interplay of rainclouds and rays of sunlight on the windy coast. Compared with earlier landscape painting, it is amazing how he divides sky and earth with an absolutely straight horizon for which the viewer is prepared by increasingly narrow, parallel strips of water, lanes and woods, painted with extreme economy of means. The grandiose skies reply to the landscape's lively rhythm of light and dark with correspondingly light and dark clouds. The Dresden painting of around 1664 is one of Koninck's major works. His contemporaries thought highly of him, particularly as a history painter and portraitist.

Jacob Isaacksz van Ruisdael

Haarlem 1628/29-Amsterdam (?) 1682

The Jewish Cemetery near Ouderkerk
Signed on left on stone: JvRuisdael
Canvas, 84 x 95 cm
First mentioned in the inventory of 1754.
Gal. no. 1502

Hardly any other Dutch landscape painting is as poetic as Ruisdael's *Jewish Cemetery*. The painter takes the liberty of moving the tombstones of the Beth Haim of Ouderkerk near Amsterdam, which were identified by name, and the ruin of Egmond Castle near Alkmaar, to a dark, wet mountain landscape shrouded in storm clouds. The ominous atmosphere of decay and death contrasts with the rainbow, a symbol of union with God and the Resurrection. Goethe was so impressed by this painting, created around 1653-55, that he described it in an essay *Ruysdael als Dichter* (Ruysdael as Poet). There is another far larger version of the painting in Detroit.

Herman Saftleven the Younger

Rotterdam 1609-Utrecht 1685

View of Utrecht
Signed lower centre on boat: HSL (ligated) 1664
Copper, 19.5 x 35.5 cm
First mentioned in the inventory of 1722-1728.
Gal. no. 1289

Unlike the landscapes by Koninck and Ruisdael, the painter of vedute set himself the task of producing views of towns that are as topographically accurate as possible. In this small panel, Saftleven depicts Utrecht from the north. The Gothic cathedral, still undamaged at that time, rises up among the predominantly Romanesque churches and monasteries. Exactly ten years later, the cathedral nave between the transept and tower was to be completely destroyed by a storm. Today, there is a large gap between the two parts of the building. Saftleven became famous for his views of the Moselle and the Rhine which were copied, in picturesque views, until well into the 19th century.

Gerrit Adriaensz Berckheyde

Haarlem 1638-Haarlem 1698

Street in Haarlem
Signed on right on bench:
G. Berck. Heyde 16.
Oak, 43 x 39 cm
Acquired in 1912. Gal. no. 1523 A

With this painting, Gerrit Berckheyde shows us a Dutch town at close range. The detail is exceeded only by Jan Vermeer in his famous *Straatje* (Rijksmuseum, Amsterdam). In this topographically accurate painting, we look into Jansstraat, in Haarlem, which leads to the north side of the Church of St Bavo. The low evening sun in the west casts wide shadows into the street and makes the red brick buildings glow warmly. This tranquil painting with its burghers' houses and shops shows the prosperity of the young Dutch Republic far more clearly than any allegorical picture.

Job Adriaensz Berckheyde

Haarlem 1630-Haarlem 1693

Interior of the Church of St Bavo in Haarlem
Signed lower right: I. Berckheyde 1665
Oak, 61.5 x 85.3 cm
Acquired in 1874. Gal. no. 1511

With this picture by Job Berckheyde, we enter the Church of St Bavo in Haarlem, the north side of which was painted by his brother Gerrit in his *Street in Haarlem* (Gal. no. 1523 A). The picture of the church's interior is a remarkably clear reproduction, resulting from an accurate observation of warm and cold light effects. The walls are unadorned. Only a few coats of arms of the deceased decorate the interior which, in accordance with Calvinist theology, should be used only to spread the word of God. The large glass window in the west, now the site of a monumental organ of 1738, illustrates an *historic* event: Emperor Frederick II adds the sword to the Haarlem coat of arms in 1219.

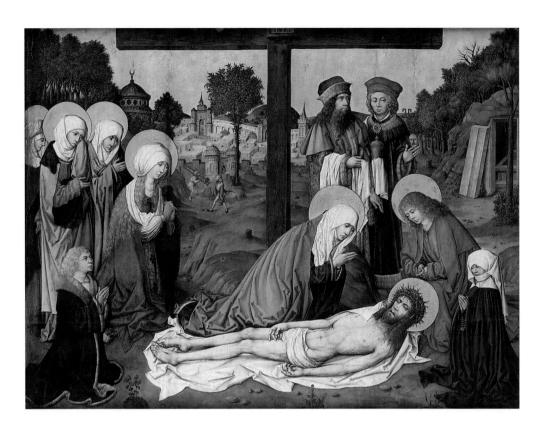

Master of the Housebook

c. 1445-1505

The Lamentation of Christ
Spruce, 131 x 171 cm
Acquired in 1903. Gal. no. 1868 A

The artist's name is derived from a Mediaeval manuscript, known as the Housebook, which contains drawings by his hand. The manuscript is now at Wolfegg Palace in southwest Germany. The artist worked in the Middle Rhine region from the 1470s, and was probably in Heidelberg around 1480. His prints and drawings in particular show Martin Schongauer's influence. They are of special significance because of their life-like portrayals and abundance of worldly motifs. The artist seems to have followed Netherlandish examples in his composition of the *Lamentation of Christ*. He portrays Christ's suffering with shocking penetration, the body being reminiscent of the naturalism of Late Gothic painted wooden sculptures. On the right and left of the panel, the donors are kneeling in adoration. They are smaller than the figures of the saints because they are less important.

Albrecht Dürer

Nuremberg 1471-Nuremberg 1528

Twelve-year-old Jesus in the Temple
Softwood, 62.5 x 45 cm
Acquired in 1588. Gal. no. 1877

The altarpiece *Seven Sorrows of the Virgin*, Dürer's first large painting after settling as master in Nuremberg, is still linked with the Late Gothic tradition. The seven paintings were originally on a single panel grouped around the figure of the *Mater Dolorosa* (today in the Alte Pinakothek, Munich). Of these, the *Twelve-year-old Jesus in the Temple* shows how his parents find him, after a long search, in serious discussion with the doctors in the temple (St Luke 2: 41-52). The *Seven Sorrows* were often contrasted with the *Seven Joys of the Virgin* surrounding a *Coronation of the Virgin*. Dürer painted the *Seven Joys*, together also almost two metres high, but these are known only from later drawings.

Albrecht Dürer

Nuremberg 1471-Nuremberg 1528

Portrait of Bernhard von Reesen
Signed with monogram AD and dated 1521
Oak, 45.5 x 31.5 cm
Acquired in 1743. Gal. no. 1871

Dürer's great importance for the development of German painting was primarily due to his ability to use and adopt foreign forms. He visited Italy twice, and the Netherlands once, where he produced this characteristic late work in 1521. According to a note in Dürer's diary, Bernhard von Reesen, the son of a respected merchant's family in Danzig, paid him eight guilders for the portrait. The subject had his portrait painted at the age of 30. This was considered the perfect age, since Christ had died and risen at the age of 30 or 33. It was widely believed that, whether you died as a child or an old man, the resurrected body would adopt that age (for example, St Augustine, *De Civitate Dei* LXXII, 15). Thus, it was thought appropriate to commission a portrait that suggested both hope and eternal life. Bernhard von Reesen died the same year that Dürer painted this impressive portrait.

117

Lucas Cranach the Elder

Kronach/Upper Franconia 1472-Weimar 1553

Duke Heinrich the Pious
Transferred from wood to canvas, 184 x 82.5 cm

Duchess Katharina of Mecklenburg
Signed lower left with winged serpent,
LC and 1514
Transferred from wood to canvas, 184 x 82.5 cm
First mentioned in the catalogue of 1920.
Gal. no. 1906 G/H

Full-length portraits were new. Standing figures of saints had previously been painted on wing panels, such as Dürer's *Paumgartner Altarpiece* with its portrait-like figures of 1502 (Alte Pinakothek, Munich), but not as independent portraits. This form of representation may have been inspired by tombs which, from an early date, had narrow plates with life-sized effigies in relief. Cranach's outstanding artistic quality, his sense of decoration and representation, are evident from these portraits of the ducal couple. Their marriage of 1512 is indicated by the wreaths of carnations in his hair and the jewellery with symbolic clasped hands.

Hans Baldung Grien

Schwäbisch-Gmünd 1484/85-Strasbourg 1545

Mucius Scaevola
Signed on right on chest:
HGBaldung Fac. 1531 (HGB ligated)
Lime wood, 98 x 68 cm
Acquired in 1927. Gal. no. 1888 B

After his initial training in Strasbourg, Hans Baldung Grien came to Nuremberg, in 1503, where he entered Dürer's workshop. After the strong influence of Dürer in early days, he turned to Mannerism of brilliant colours and great expressive power. This painting of an episode of Rome's history dates from this period. Mucius wanted to assassinate the Etruscan king, Porsenna, as he was besieging Rome, but stabbed his paymaster by mistake. Captured and threatened with death, Mucius Scaevola demonstrated his fearlessness by holding his hand over a basin of burning coals. When he said that 300 fellow Romans would follow his example, he so impressed Porsenna that the Etruscan king made peace – an *Exemplum Virtutis*, therefore, for an ideal and courageous people (Livy II, 12 seq; Plutarch IV, 17).

Hans Holbein the Younger   ▷

Augsburg 1497/98-London 1543

Portrait of Charles de Solier, Sieur de Morette
Oak, 92.5 x 75.5 cm
Acquired in 1746. Gal. no. 1890

Charles de Solier, Sieur de Morette (1480/81-1564), was in state services under four French kings. On several occasions he was the French envoy to England, for example from April 1534 to July 1535 when this portrait was painted. Holbein depicts every minute detail, including his subject's clothing and jewellery, but the dominant impression is achieved by the strictly frontal composition which holds all the details in a firm structure. »If there has ever been a portrait of eternal value, this is it ...« wrote Karoline Schlegel of the picture, which was in 1799, believed to be a work of Leonardo da Vinci until 1846. Holbein was to paint a similar block-like portrait of Henry VIII five years later. He was court painter in England from 1536.

Joseph Heintz the Elder

Basle 1564-Prague 1609

The Rape of Persephone
Copper, 63 x 94 cm
First mentioned in the Guarienti inventory
(1747-1750).
Gal. no. 1971

Together with Bartholomäus Spranger and
Hans von Aachen, Joseph Heintz belonged to
the main group of Rudolfine Mannerists who
worked at the court of Prague to satisfy the
very personal taste in art of Emperor Rudolf
II. All of them had been trained in Italy where
the bases for their virtuoso, excessively fine
style are to be found in models from Antiquity
to Parmigianino. The colourfulness of the
painting, which originates from Rudolf's
Kunstkammer, is dominated by a transparent
blue-green. Combined with the shimmering
mother-of-pearl flesh colour of the figures, this
creates a costly and highly nuanced effect. The
contrast between the dainty movements of the
girls from whose midst Pluto, the god of the
underworld, carries away Persephone, and the
galloping horses, is a further Mannerist characteristic (theme from Ovid's *Metamorphoses*
V, 391 seqq).

Johann Heinrich Schönfeld

Biberach an der Riss 1609-Augsburg 1682/83

Entertainment at the Spinet
Signed lower centre: J H Schönfeldt Fecit.
Monogram on spinet: JHS: Fecit (JHS linked)
Canvas, 124 x 92.5 cm
Acquired in 1741. Gal. no. 1991

The character of this painting of around 1670 is not determined by the small figures at the spinet, but by the Mannerist room with its high walls, by the interior of the gallery. The picture on the far wall has been identified as the *Battle of the Giants*, painted by Schönfeld around 1650 and also in the Dresden collection until 1945. However, Schönfeld enlarged it enormously in the gallery picture in order to stress that this is a fictitious room. The inscription »VIRTVTIS DOCVMENTO« (examples of virtue) in the lunette above the picture seems to be the leitmotif for the other battle scenes on the walls. When Schönfeld's painting reached the Vršovec Collection in Prague, Jan Onghers painted a pendant there, after 1691, which shows a gallery only of religious pictures (Gal. no. 1992). Schönfeld's highly personal style is based on Late Mannerist works and the great experience he had gained during his eighteen years in Italy.

Christoph Paudiss

Hamburg (?) c. 1625-Freising 1666

Portrait of an Old Man with Fur Hat
Signed lower left: Christoffer Paudiß. 1654
Lime wood, 51.5 x 42 cm
First mentioned in the inventory of 1722-1728.
Gal. no. 1993

In the 17th century, German painters travelled
to major art centres in other countries to perfect their skills, and often stayed there when
they had little chance of earning a living at
home. The northern German artist Paudiss
went to the Netherlands, entering Rembrandt's workshop in Amsterdam in 1642.
Paudiss continued to be influenced by Rembrandt, even when he had developed his own
style in Hungary, Dresden, Vienna and Frei-
sing. This painting of 1654 is a direct successor of Rembrandt's studies of heads which
usually showed old men, and often Jews or
Orientals. The artist was aiming not so much
at the faithful reproduction of an individual as
at an interesting interpretation of character.

Christian Seybold

Mainz 1703-Vienna 1768

Old Woman with Green Scarf
Copper, 41.5 x 32.5 cm
First mentioned in the Guarienti inventory
(1747-1750).
Gal. no. 2095

This is an extraordinarily detailed study of a
head; a miniature in which every pore, every
wrinkle and every hair seems to be painted.
Gerard Dou, one of Rembrandt's pupils and
successors, had painted heads of old men and
women, in small formats, their wrinkly skin
being created by the texture of the paint. This
picture is like a duplicate of a person, as if modelled in wax. It also displays an interest in human physiognomy, as was considered in trea-
tises at that time. The self-taught Seybold was
»Imperial Court Painter« in Vienna from 1749
and must have known the cabinet picture of
an *Old Woman* by Balthasar Denner, the most
famous painter of such works. Denner's painting, guarded like a jewel, had been bought by
Emperor Karl VI in 1726. Seybold's painting
went missing in 1945, but has recently re-
turned to the Dresden Gallery.

Johann Heinrich Roos

Reitpoldskirchen (Palatinate) 1631-Frankfurt
am Main 1685

Shepherds and Herds Beneath Rocks
Signed lower right on stone: JHRoos. fecit.
(JHR ligated)
Canvas, 59 x 79 cm
First mentioned in the inventory of 1722-1728.
Gal. no. 2002

Sandrart reports that, as a child, Roos came to
Amsterdam with his parents when they fled
the horrors of the Thirty Years' War. There he
received his artistic training before returning
to Germany around 1651/52. There is no evidence that he travelled to Rome, as has often
been suggested. In 1667, he settled in Frankfurt where he created this landscape in 1681.
His paintings display clearly his training by the
Netherlandish group of Italian-style painters
who had specialized in landscapes with southern light, ruins of Antiquity and shepherd
scenes. They include several artists (such as the
famous Albert Cuyp) who had never been to
Italy. At a later date, one of Johann Heinrich
Roos' sons, known as »Rosa di Tivoli«, was
to cause a sensation in Italy with animal paintings.

Christian Wilhelm Ernst Dietrich

Weimar 1712-Dresden 1774

Shepherdesses and Shepherds at a
Round Stone Monument
Signed: Dietricy Pinx. 1751
Canvas, 54.5 x 72.5 cm
First mentioned in the inventory of 1754.
Gal. no. 2122

Dietrich was a master in imitating other paint-ers. He created works in the style of artists as different as Rembrandt, Griffier, Van Goyen or Watteau, varying their paintings and thus clearly showing his own language. This is prob-ably more obvious to us than it was to his contemporaries. In 1731, he was appointed painter to the Saxon court, in 1746 inspector and restorer of the Dresden Gallery. In many of the details, his painting of 1751 is reminis-cent of works by Johann Heinrich Roos, al-though he uses far fuller colours and the fig-ures display the elegance of the Rococo. In view of the relief with the drunken Silenus, the painting could show the childhood of Bacchus – in the centre – on the Indian Mount Nysa where he was fed on milk by nymphs (Ovid, *Metamorphoses* III, 314 seq).

Johann Alexander Thiele

Erfurt 1685-Dresden 1752

View of Dresden from the Lössnitzhöhen
Signed lower centre: ... gemahlt von Alex. Thielen.
1751.
Canvas, 103 x 156 cm
First mentioned in the 1863 catalogue.
Gal. no. 3181

»A particularly fine prospect seen from the top of a vine-clad hill not far from Wackerbarths Ruhe. Facing Dresden and Königstein ...« is how Thiele describes the painting. It shows the valley of the river Elbe with the Lössnitz vineyards in the foreground, and Dresden sketched in the distance. Thiele, who had accepted the thirteen-year-old Dietrich as pupil in 1725, began to paint prospects influenced by panorama painting. He drew together individual characteristic points of orientation in the landscape so that he could fit a panorama onto a surface of 100 x 150 cm. However contrived the view may be, Thiele knew how to capture the hazy atmosphere in the valley, which seeps into every contour.

Anton Raphael Mengs

Aussig 1728-Rome 1779

Self-portrait in Red Coat
Pastels on paper, 55 x 42 cm
First mentioned in the 1765 catalogue.
Gal. no. P 167

Mengs was painter to the Saxon court from 1744, but he was more often in Rome than in Dresden. His education was geared to venerating the Italian Renaissance, the basis of his classicistic view of art. »His father wanted him to dress and behave as Raphael of Urbino is painted«, remarked Carl Heinrich von Heinecken of the self-portrait of the barely sixteen-year-old artist. In Rome, Mengs was friends with Winckelmann, and throughout Europe he was celebrated as a theorist and painter. His programmatic writings »On Beauty« were published in 1762. That same year, as newly appointed painter to the court of Spain, he met the old master of the Late Baroque, Giovanni Battista Tiepolo, in Madrid. A comparison of the two painters shows clearly the contrasting styles of the two epochs.

Anton Graff

Winterthur (Switzerland) 1736-Dresden 1813

Self-portrait at the Age of 58
Canvas, 168 x 105 cm
First mentioned in the 1835 catalogue.
Gal. no. 2167

This painting of 1794/95 demonstrates the full range of Graff's artistic skills. The complicated turn towards the viewer and the representation of the entire figure, in a large format, underline the exceptional character of the work. It contrasts with Graff's otherwise typical half-length or three-quarter portraits. The painting expresses the artist's justified pride as a recognized portraitist. He had introduced himself in Dresden, in 1766, with a *Self-portrait* (Gal. no. 2166), resulting in his appointment as court painter. In 1788 he became Professor of Portrait Painting at the Academy. He painted numerous portraits, including many of the leading personalities of the Age of Enlightenment, the classical and romantic periods.

Christian Leberecht Vogel (?)

Dresden 1759-Dresden 1816

Child with Doll
Canvas, 48 x 43 cm
Acquired in 1937. Gal. no. 2189 B

Christian Leberecht Vogel, a pupil of Schenau, became Professor at the Dresden Academy of Art in 1814, having been painter to the noble von Solms family at Wildenfels Palace near Zwickau. His portraits of children are extremely popular. The *Child with Doll* is particularly attractive because of the artist's use of a painted frame through which the delicate child with large eyes smiles at us. He thus creates the illusion that both the bird cage and the doll, in particular, are in the same room as the viewer. The picture looks so typical of the Biedermeier period (1815-30) that the attribution to Vogel is by no means certain. The painting thus ushers in the 19th century which continues in the Dresden Gallery of Modern Masters.

Index of Artists Illustrated